TO THE

Rev. William Gorsuch Rowland, M.A.

MINISTER AND OFFICIAL OF

THE ROYAL PECULIAR OF ST. MARY'S, SHREWSBURY,

AND PREBENDARY OF LICHFIELD,

AS A HUMBLE BUT SINCERE TESTIMONY OF RESPECT,

FOR HIS ZEALOUS AND MUNIFICENT EXERTIONS

IN RESTORING AND HEIGHTENING

THE BEAUTIES AND ARCHITECTURE OF SEVERAL OF THE

CHURCHES IN THIS TOWN,

AND FOR HIS

UNWEARIED ATTENTION TO MANY OF OUR

PUBLIC INSTITUTIONS,

The Memorials of Shrewsbury

ARE VERY RESPECTFULLY INSCRIBED,

BY

HIS OBEDIENT SERVANT,

HENRY PIDGEON.

MEMORIALS

OF

SHREWSBURY:

BEING A

CONCISE DESCRIPTION OF THE TOWN

AND ITS ENVIRONS,

Adapted as

𝔄 𝔊eneral 𝔊uide

FOR THE

INFORMATION OF VISITORS AND RESIDENTS.

BY

HENRY PIDGEON.

ILLUSTRATED WITH THIRTY-SIX ENGRAVINGS.

"FLOREAT SALOPIA."

Shrewsbury:

PRINTED BY JOHN EDDOWES, CORN MARKET.

1837.

This publication is a limited edition and has been reproduced in facsimile from the original publication of 1837.

Printed at the Shirehall, Shrewsbury

I.S.B.N. : 0 903802 00 7

PREFACE.

A little Manual adapted to assist the enquiring stranger in his perambulation around Shrewsbury having been long required, an ardent attachment to his native place, and compliance with the wishes of many friends whose opinions demand respect, are circumstances that have induced the present writer to undertake the task, in which he has been materially assisted by the possession of several volumes of SALOPIAN ANNALS, or memoranda of all the principal events that have occurred in the town for several past years, the collection whereof has afforded him a pleasing recreation in those scraps of time snatched from active professional avocations—periods wherein every one has his favourite pursuit, and in which any individual may, by prudently employing them for his own pleasure, not unfrequently render himself useful to others.

It may be further stated that the present design is purely patriotic ; and whilst no expence has been spared in the numerous embellishments, candour and truth (combined with accuracy and conciseness) have been carefully observed throughout a more extensive field of local information and graphical illustration than has heretofore been cultivated in any previous work adapted as a Guide through the Metropolis of Shropshire,—many subjects being now classified and brought under general notice for the first time.

The Author would therefore hope that the MEMORIALS OF SHREWSBURY will be found to afford a comprehensive and faithful illustration to the stranger of whatever may be important in this ancient and beautifully situated town, as well as useful and deserving the confidence of his fellow-townsmen in particular, to whom he offers them (to use the words of our great lexicographer) " in the spirit of a man that has endeavoured well," and with the utmost sincerity for the best interests of his native place.

H. P.

High-street, 1836.

ILLUSTRATIONS,

FROM DRAWINGS MADE EXPRESSLY FOR THIS WORK.

PAGE.

CONTENTS.

CONTENTS.

CONTENTS.

CONTENTS.

SHREWSBURY.

Admir'd SALOPIA! that with venial pride
   Eyes her bright form in Severn's ambient wave;
Fam'd for her loyal cares in perils tried;
   Her daughters lovely and her striplings brave.

SHENSTONE.

Memorials of Shrewsbury.

SITUATION.

"A precious stone set in silver."

SHAKSPEARE.

THE Town of SHREWSBURY stands nearly in the centre of the county of which it is the capital; it is situated on two gentle declivities, and is formed by the river Severn into a peninsula, somewhat in the shape of a horse-shoe, having an isthmus not more than three hundred yards across.

A variety of opinions have prevailed as to who made choice of the commanding situation and natural retreat which the town affords, as well as to the period of its foundation.

It has been stated to be of far prior date than the ancient Uriconium (the present Wroxeter), from the circumstances that it was the custom of the Romans to throw up stations, and to make roads parallel or adjacent to British camps. One thing however is certain, that no vestige of that imperial people has been discovered within its precinct.

The truth is conceived to be, that Shrewsbury was occupied or built some time in the fifth century, after the destruction of the Roman Uriconium, as a place where the fugitive Britons might find an asylum from the devastations of their Saxon invaders.

ETYMOLOGY.

The Britons gave the place the appellation of *Pengwern*, the Saxons *Scrobbes-byrig ;* both are synonymous, importing a fenced eminence covered with shrubs. The ancient Welsh called it, and do so to this day, *Ammwythig*, signifying "The Delight." The Normans *Sciropesberie*, and subsequently *Salopesberie* and *Schrosbury*, from whence is formed its present name Shrewsbury and Salop. The antiquary Leland thus beautifully accounts for its name :

> Edita Pengwerni late fastigia splendent,
> Urbs sita lunato veluti mediamnis in orbe,
> Colle tumet modico; duplici quoque ponte superbit :
> Accipiens patria sibi lingua nomen ab alnis.

which may be thus translated—

> Built on a hill, fair SALOF greets the eye,
> While Severn like an eel curves gliding by :
> Two bridges cross the bark-conveying stream,
> And British alders gave the town a name.

ANCIENT HISTORY.

When the Britons had become somewhat settled in their new possessions, they built themselves a city, which (as has been already stated) was called *Pengwern*. After its destruction under Cynddylan, we find Pengwern inhabited by a King of Powis,—the capital of his kingdom, and ranking among the twenty-eight cities of Britain.

Brochwel Yscithrog, or the tusked, King of Powis, whom the Saxon Chronicle calls the Earlderman of the Britons, retained possession of a great part of Shropshire. and fixed his residence in Pengwern, about 617; his palace being where the ruins of Old St. Chad's Church now stand.

Eliseg, his sixth descendant, recovered the portion of his " inheritance of Powis" from the Saxons, by the sword, during the reign of the Mercian King Offa, which continued from 755 to 794, but being unable to maintain it, he surrendered by treaty to the Saxons, whereby Pengwern lost the dignity of a metropolis.

Of the state of our town under its native princes we have no information: the arts of civil life, in which the Britons had improved, under their Roman masters, were probably lost during the almost constant warfare of three centuries. This we may reasonably conclude was the case, from the appellation given to it by the new possessors, *Scrobbes-byrig*, a fenced eminence, but overgrown with shrubs.

Nothing is related of the town during the period it formed a portion of the Mercian territory, though the place doubtless experienced the many revolutions of that kingdom.

In the reign of Alfred, Scrobbes-byrig was numbered among the principal cities of Britain. Ethelred the Unready, having been pursued by the Danes, kept his Christmas here in 1006, and in the next year resigned the government of Mercia unto his son-in-law Ædric, who made this town his occasional residence.

Under the Saxon monarchs the town must have been of importance to possess the privilege of a mint, which it retained for a considerable period, many coins of which are extant.

Ædric Sylvaticus, or the Forester, in conjunction with Owen Gwynedd, Prince of North Wales, laid siege to the town in 1068; but William the First sending two earls to the relief of the castle, the rebels burned a portion of the town and withdrew: the king however speedily revenged the insult with much slaughter.

The Saxons were removed from all places of trust by the Norman Conqueror, who rewarded his principal adherents with portions of their lands. He conferred upon his kinsman, Roger de Montgomery, the earldom of Shrewsbury, to which he added a grant of the town and ample domains in the county.

In 1138, the nation being divided as to Stephen's right to the crown, that monarch laid siege to the castle. Fitz Alan, the governor, favouring the Empress Maud, fled, and Stephen, who had conducted the siege in his own person, was so exasperated at the obstinacy of the besieged, who resolutely held out nearly four weeks, that he put ninety-three of them to an ignominious death.

From the border situation of Shrewsbury to a hostile country, it was considered of much importance to our early monarchs, and consequently became the scene of many a negotiation and contest with the Welsh, whose frequent incursions were most harassing.

The Princes of North Wales having been long uneasy neighbours to the Kings of England, John thought it expedient to hold a council here to make a treaty with Llewelyn the Great, the then Prince of Wales. In the year 1202 the king gave Llewelyn his natural daughter Joanna in marriage; and, as if in gratitude to his father-in-law, he soon recommenced hostilities against him, and marched with a numerous body of his vigorous subjects from the Cambrian wilds to Shrewsbury, which he succeeded in taking without much resistance.

The town, however, did not long continue under the subjection or possession of its new masters, they being dispossessed by Henry III. who on more than one occasion kept his court here.

In 1234, Richard, Earl Marescall, being told that Henry intended to seize him when he repaired to parliament, fled to Llewelyn, and they both appeared before Shrewsbury with a powerful army, and burned part of the suburb of Frankwell, returning to the mountains laden with the spoil of the inhabitants, many of whom they had barbarously murdered.

Henry III. with his forces again marched to Shrewsbury in 1241, where he remained a fortnight, when David relinquished all lands Llewelyn had seized from the late king in the war between him and his barons.

In 1256, Henry, wishing probably to attach himself in the favour of the burgesses, in order to make their town a bulwark against Wales, granted them two new charters on the same day; he likewise summoned his army here; and in 1260 great activity was evinced in fortifying the town, in consequence of a rupture which was speedily expected from the aggression of the Welsh Prince.

Edward the First resided here in 1277, whither he transferred some of the supreme courts of justice. In 1282 David joined Llewelyn, who again took up arms, which compelled Edward to return to Shrewsbury with his courts, where he had assembled his army, which remained some months.

David, the last of the princes of the Ancient Britons, having at length become a prisoner in the hands of Edward in 1283, was sent in chains to Shrewsbury, where a parliament was assembled to meet Sept. 30th, being "*the first national convention in which the Commons had any share by legal authority*." Twenty cities and towns, Shrewsbury being one, were directed to send two deputies, and every high sheriff to send two knights. It is supposed they met in the chapter house, or refectory of the abbey, where David was tried and cruelly condemned to be dragged at a horse's tail through the streets of Shrewsbury, and to be afterwards hung and cut down while alive, his heart and bowels burnt before his face, his body quartered, and his head sent to London to accompany that of his brother Llewelyn.

Revenge, it may be said, is sweet; but how often does it occur that the gratification of resentment over a fallen enemy transmits his encomium to posterity.

The town, being strongly fenced, was visited by Edward in 1322, where he was honourably received by the inhabitants, who went out to meet him clad in armour; he continued here for several days, about which time many of the nobility had assembled to witness a grand tournament.

Richard II. Jan. 29th, 1397-8, adjourned his parliament from Westminster to Shrewsbury, which was denominated the "GREAT PARLIAMENT," from the important state affairs which were transacted in it. The cross of Canterbury was brought here, upon which the lords spiritual and temporal were sworn to observe and keep all the statutes which were then made. Chester was on this occasion made a principality, and several oppressive laws enacted, which afterwards formed some of the accusations against Richard by Henry of Bolingbroke, when he usurped the throne.

The revolution which placed Henry of Lancaster on the throne seems to have met the approbation of the inhabitants; for when the Duke ostensibly proceeded into Wales to please Richard, he was nobly received here.

After the death of Richard, Owen Glendower, concerning whose birth the muse of Shakspeare says—

> " The frame and foundation of the earth
>   Shak'd like a coward"—

asserted his pretensions to the two ancient principalities of North Wales and Powis, and pursued his claim with undaunted courage, added to a strong resentment for the contumely with which his demands, public and private, had been treated by the successor of the unfortunate Richard, to whom he was a firm and unshaken friend. On the 20th of September, 1400, he boldly caused himself to be proclaimed Prince of Wales, and infested the Marches with a strong body of Welshmen, who maintained a warfare against the governing authorities. In this he was subsequently supported by the Earl of Northumberland, headed by his son, the valiant Henry Percy, surnamed Hotspur, who being assisted by the Earl of Worcester and a numerous force of Scottish troops under the command of Earl Douglas, agreed to meet Glendower at Shrewsbury. Henry, being made acquainted with their movements, hastened with all speed to secure this important town, and arrived here July 21st, 1403, just in time to hoist his banner on the walls, and thereby secure the stability of his crown, having but a few hours' march of Percy and his advanced guard.

On the morning of the 22d, the memorable BATTLE OF SHREWSBURY commenced; the skirmishing began under the walls of the Castle Gates, but the principal scene of action was about three miles distant, at a place called BATTLEFIELD. The armies on both sides amounted, it is said, to 40,000, and the contest was severe and sanguinary. Fate, however, decided that the efforts of Henry against this powerful faction should be victorious—a faction, which, having contributed to place him on the seat of government, now sought to dethrone him. The king is recorded to have fought with an ardour worthy the crown he was defending, and the spear of his warlike son, the future hero of Agincourt, did wonders. In fact it was one of the most decisive battles recorded in early English history.

Upwards of 2000 nobles, knights, and gentlemen, and 6000 private soldiers, are said to have fallen in the engagement.

Most of the dead bodies were buried on the spot, over whom Henry, in gratitude for his victory, piously erected a college of secular canons to pray for the souls of the slain. The more distinguished were interred in the Dominican and Augustine Friaries of the town.

The gallant Hotspur was discovered among the slain covered with wounds, and dispatched to Shrewsbury, where Henry satiated his revenge by the ignominy of dismembering the lifeless remains, the head and quarters of which were exhibited over the gate at York, and afterwards delivered to his wife for interment. The Earl of Worcester, Sir Richard Vernon, &c. were beheaded.

Shakspeare, in his Henry the Fourth, has given vividness and immortality to this battle, and humourously peopled it with heroes of the most fanciful description.

The Cambrian chieftain, Glendower, with an army of 12,000 men, marched as far as Oswestry, and was by some means unable to arrive in time to join in the action; for had he reached ere the king's forces were victorious, the result might have terminated very differently for the king and his valiant son. Gough states a tradition, that Glendower proceeded to Shelton, and ascended a lofty oak (the trunk of which is still remaining near the Oswestry road), from whence he might reconnoitre and gain the earliest intelligence of the event of the battle.

The royal blood of this noble Welshman was in no respect chilled by the defeat of his confederates, for in the next year he carried his ravages even to the gates of the Welsh Bridge, destroying much of the suburb of Frankwell and several townships in the vicinity.

In 1460, Edward IV. marched with an army of 23,000 men from this town to the battle of Mortimer's Cross, and he chose this place for the residence of his queen, where she was delivered of her second and third sons, Richard and George Plantagenet.

On the landing of the Earl of Richmond, afterwards King Henry the Seventh, at Milford Haven, in August, 1485, he determined to march for Shrewsbury. On his arriving at the Welsh Bridge he found the place in a posture of defence, the gates closed against him, and the bailiffs within ready to give their answer. On his demanding admittance as their rightful king, a curious MS. records that the chief bailiff, Thomas Mytton, replied—" He knew no king but Richard, whose bailiffs he and his fellow were, upon which he swore that the earl should not enter there but over his belly." On this, Richmond returned and passed the night at Forton Heath, where his army was encamped. He, however, succeeded the next morning ; and Mr. Mytton, in order to conform with the letter of his oath, laid himself down on the ground, and permitted the earl to step over him, whereupon the portcullis of the bridge was drawn up, and the earl with his retinue were admitted, to the general joy of the inhabitants, notwithstanding it went *against the stomach* of the " stoute wyse gentilman, Maister Myttoon."

In Shrewsbury Richmond was first proclaimed king, and raised soldiers, but left the bailiffs to pay them. He lodged in a house on the Wyle Cop (three doors below the Lion Inn), from whence he marched to Bosworth Field, where the engagement took place which deprived Richard III. of his throne and his life.

Henry VII. visited the town in 1490, with his queen, and son (Prince Arthur), and kept the feast of St. George in the collegiate church of St. Chad ; they made another visit in 1495, and were sumptuously entertained by the corporation.

At the general dissolution of monasteries, in 1539, it appears to have been the intention of Henry VIII. to form thirteen new bishopricks,* one of which was to have been at Shrewsbury.   Browne Willis states that John Boucher, Abbot of Leicester, was actually nominated " BISHOP OF SHREWSBURY ;"—hence the tradition, as our historians remark, so gratifying to the pride of every true Salopian, that their forefathers had the offer of having their borough converted into a city, but that they preferred inhabiting the FIRST OF TOWNS.

1551. The spring of this year was fatally distinguished by the commencement of a dreadful epidemic in this town, called the " sweating sickness."

During the reign of Queen Elizabeth, Sir Henry Sidney, President of Wales and Lord Deputy of Ireland, visited this town almost annually, and was always received with the highest respect; his celebrated son, Sir Philip, was educated at our Free Schools.   Sir Henry, as Knight of the Garter, kept the feast of St. George here, in 1581, with great splendour.   He marched in state from his residence, the Council House, to St. Chad's Church, the stalls of which were decorated with the arms of the knights, divine service being " sung by note."   On the 1st of May, the four masters of the schools entertained his lordship with a costly

* Our ancestors petitioned the king for permission to convert the monastery of Salop into " a college, or free school."

banquet, and on the following day three hundred and sixty of the scholars assembled in the " Gay," several of whom addressed him in speeches. He departed on the 8th, by water, "taking his bardge under the Castle," when another pageant took place on the island near the Horse Ferry.

Shrewsbury was a favourite retreat for Charles I. during the troublous period of his reign, and he was frequently received by the inhabitants with every feeling of loyalty and attachment. He established a mint here, and kept his court at the Council House. In the year 1642, he drew up his army on a spot afterwards called the " SOLDIER'S PIECE," and which is now used as a race ground, where he delivered an harangue to them and the chief gentlemen of the county, who had in his time of need rendered him pecuniary assistance and service.

The town was taken by storm in 1644-5, under the command of Colonels Mytton and Bowyer, of the parliamentary army, the inhabitants experiencing all the vicissitudes of a siege, in the plunder of their goods and destruction of property. An attempt was made, in 1654, to surprise it, in favour of the restoration of monarchy, by Sir Thomas Harries, but the scheme, although deeply planned, was frustrated.

James II. in the month of August, 1687, kept his Court at the Council House, and was attended by many of the nobility and gentry of the county, on which occasion, it is said, "the conduits ran with wine," and other most liberal entertainments and rejoicings welcomed the royal guest. At the same time he graciously received a purse of one hundred guineas, which was presented to him by the munificence of the corporation.

The inhabitants on many occasions have been thus foremost to testify loyalty to their sovereign.

In 1715 their adherence to the House of Hanover was strongly manifested by voluntarily raising a body of horse and foot for the protection of the town, and placing the walls and gates (then entire) in a position of defence.

At the time also apprehensions were entertained of the Pretender and the Scottish invasion in 1745, a regiment of foot was raised here for the service of government; and, subsequently, a militia and cavalry have been embodied.

In the year 1832, the most lively enthusiasm was displayed on the entrance into Shrewsbury of Her Royal Highness the Duchess of Kent and the Princess Victoria, heir presumptive to the British throne.

From the foregoing cursory glance given to the leading events of our ancient history, it may be necessary to remark that it would have been less difficult to the writer could he have extended his observations as to particular occurrences; but the nature of the work being a notice of the *present* rather than of the *past* state of the place, brevity of description in this, as in some other portions, will be indispensible.

But the numerous features of historical and antiquarian interest which the town affords, its BRITISH and SAXON state, the destiny of its NORMAN EARLS, its SIEGE BY STEPHEN, the UNION OF WALES to the English Crown, the Formation of Parliaments, the BATTLE OF SHREWSBURY and Fall of Hotspur, the numerous VISITS OF ROYALTY, the Entrance and PROCLAMATION OF HENRY VII. the Commencement of the CIVIL WAR in the Time of Charles I. and Meetings of the COUNCIL OF THE MARCHES OF WALES, while forming constituent parts of our national story, are especially connected with this town, and will be found amply detailed in the valuable History of Shrewsbury published by the late Reverend Messrs. Owen and Blakeway, where everything difficult in civil and ecclesiastical localities is explained in a scientific and masterly manner, and with the greatest discrimination.

THE CASTLE.

" But time   *   *   *
Has seen this ruin'd pile complete,
Big with the vanity of state."

SCOTT.

The civil history of the town being somewhat connected with the Castle, a notice of that edifice will properly occupy this place.

After the Earldom of Shrewsbury had been given by William the Conquerer to Roger de Montgomery, one of his first works was the building of a stately Castle, or, rather, the enlargement of a previous one, which it is certain existed here anterior to the Norman Conquest, on that narrow isthmus where the town is undefended by the river.

This is supposed to have taken place about the year 1070, on a site previously occupied by fifty-one houses, and was a measure of necessity, in order to restrain the hostile incursions of the Welsh, to which the town, from its situation near the borders, was frequently exposed ; and having probably received injury from the siege two

c

years previous, and being also limited in size, was inadequate to the dignity of a wealthy earl, who enjoyed the feudal supremacy of nearly the whole of Shropshire.

The Castle, in succession, was possessed by the two sons of the founder, until the reign of Henry I. when it became a royal fortress, under the custody of a constable.

Edward I. introduced a new style of castellated archichitecture; the stronger portion, therefore, now remaining was probably erected by direction of that monarch, being in the style generally adopted during his reign.

On the union of Wales it was no longer important as a place of defence, and the building began gradually to decay, although in the civil war it was repaired and garrisoned for the king, and afterwards escaped the almost general demolition of royal fortresses by its surrender to the parliamentary army in 1645.

The Castle subsequently reverted to the burgesses, who resigned it to Charles II. and that monarch presented it to Lord Newport.   It is now the property of the Duke of Cleveland, and is occupied by J. C. Pelham, Esq. one of the members for the borough.

The present remains have a picturesque effect, and are composed of a deep red stone.   They consist of the keep, the walls of the inner court, and the great semi-circular arch of

THE INTERIOR GATEWAY,

from which the last Norman Earl of Shrewsbury issued with the keys of the gates to make submission to Henry I. Although the masonry of the jambs of this noble gateway is singularly irregular, it has, through a period of nearly 800 years, retained its strength unshaken amid the ravages of time and war.   It was formerly defended by a portcullis and towers.

The keep consists of two large round towers, embattled and pierced, connected by a square building of about 100 feet in length.

The interior is much altered from its original appearance, and now forms a handsome private residence, modern pointed windows having been placed therein when it was repaired by Sir William Pulteney, about the close of the last century. The drawing room is supposed to have been

c 2

the guard chamber in the time of Charles I. The castle still retains one mark of its ancient dignity, for in the area of the inner court the knights of the shire are nominated, and when the result of the election is declared, are girt with their swords by the Sheriff. On the north-east side of this court is a postern, built in the time of Charles I. ; and the battlements of the western wall have an interior platform, and are curiously pierced with narrow eyelets for the convenience of the cross-bowmen, around which time has wove its ivy mantling.

On the south side within the court is a mount,* rising upwards of 100 feet above the bed of the river. The summit is surrounded by a wall, and crowned by a watch tower, which forms a bold and beautiful object. The tower was rebuilt during the repair of the castle, from a design and under the superintendance of the late Thomas Telford, Esq. who was then residing with Sir William Pulteney. In this elevated tower Mr. Telford wrote the beautiful poem to his countryman Burns, and thus alludes to its site near the river Severn :—

> No distant Swiss with warmer glow
> E'er heard his native music flow,
> Nor could his wishes stronger grow
>   Than still have mine ;
> When up this ancient mount I go
>   With songs of thine.

The sides of the mount are richly planted, and the summit commands a view of unrivalled beauty, with the most extensive amphitheatre of mountains of which perhaps the island can boast, inclosing within its wide sweep an eminently fertile, finely wooded, and beautifully diversified champagne country. 'Tis here that, after the eye has wandered from object to object, from the foreground to the most

* This was an essential characteristic of the castellated structure of the Danes, although subsequently adopted by the Normans.

extreme distance with delight, that the words of *Thomson* naturally occur, as if written upon such a spot—

> " Oh, scene surpassing fable, and yet true !"

It is now difficult to form an adequate idea of the original extent of this fortress; but it is certain that the castle formerly occupied a much larger space than is now marked out by its walls, the ballium (or outer court) extending within the town probably as far as the water-lane. The northern and north eastern sides were defended by a deep ditch or vallum encompassing the base of the bold and natural elevation on which the castle stands, having a communication with the river, but it is now filled up and forms a thoroughfare.

The remains of a duplicate rampart is distinguishable on the western side; and other outworks and towers might have stood near the front of the present county gaol, the Severn being a protection towards the east.

> In auncient tyme our elders had desire,
> To buyld their townes on steepe and stately hill;
> To shewe that as their hearts did still aspyre,
> So should their works declare their worthie will.
>
> CHURCHYARD.

THE FEUDAL STATE

of Shrewsbury carries with it associations of imposing importance;—seated upon a hill rising from a noble ambient river, it was thus doubly fortified by nature; while art, with

no unsparing hand, had raised an almost impregnable rampart of stone, flanked by many towers and gates.*

The imagination will thus readily picture CAER PEN-
GWERN : the woody eminence, with its curiously wrought
buildings and domestic mansions ranged in irregular groups,
surmounted by lofty spires and embattled turrets, irradiated
by the effulgence of the meridian sun, or catching the last
smiles of his departing ray,—a commanding castle on the
narrow isthmus, with its stately towers and formidable walls,
frowning in august pride high above the surrounding plain,
—solitary convents, crested with pinnacles and gables, in
the verdant meadows on the margin of the rolling stream,
over which strongly fortified bridges with massive portcullis
and towers, afforded a defence from hostile invaders.

This faint retrospect must kindle in the mind consider-
ations of the progress and fluctuations of science and taste,
—the character, condition, and habits of men in these
times,—with the works done " in their days and in the old
time before them ;"—while the contemplation thereof
cannot fail of exciting gratitude to the SUPREME GIVER,
for the security we *now* enjoy, without the precaution of
barbican and battlements.

* The town had originally three principal gates, besides several postern
or smaller gates, and was from an early period encompassed with a wall,
strengthened by towers in those parts most liable to be attacked. Within the
last sixty years many parts of the walls have been built upon, and the gates
and towers, with one exception, fallen a prey, not so much to the ruthless
power of time, as to the less sparing enemy—modern improvement.

PRESENT STATE.

"A lovely spot
For all that life can ask! Salubrious! mild!
Its hills are green; its woods and prospects fair;
Its meadows fertile!"

COTTLE'S ALFRED.

The bold situation of the town, girdled by the health-bearing breezes of a beauteous river, with an eminence crown'd by aspiring temples,

That upward cast their golden vanes, and shine
A bright tiara,

gives a striking and majestic appearance to Shrewsbury.

When seen from most parts of the adjacent country the town forms a delightful object,—a gem encircled by a paradise;—new beauties and charming views being continually produced by the pre-eminent spires and towers; whilst the effect in the background is much heightened by an extensive range of noble mountains, which diversify the prospect, and add interest to the rich and picturesque landscape.

The exterior of the town is in most parts separated from the river by a portion of garden and meadow ground, skirted by a line of genteel houses, which command delightful prospects of the adjoining country.

As a place of residence Shrewsbury has long been considered highly eligible, from its elevated and beautiful situation, the salubrity and general healthfulness of its air, the natural dryness of the soil, the agreeable drives and promenades by which it is surrounded, and (what is equally important) the excellence and purity of its water.

Many parts of the environs have been justly recommended as suitable to valetudinarians who may visit Shrewsbury from North Wales and other parts, to avail themselves of the able medical assistance which it possesses, and who are, as it were, enticed by the agreeableness and variety of the scenery to a salutary and necessary exercise.

The interior of the town presents several curious and interesting specimens of the domestic architecture of our ancestors; the projecting bay windows, fanciful antique carving, mouldings, &c. display a singular appearance in contrast with the more modern habitations, in many of which the taste of their respective proprietors is effectively evinced.

The streets, as in most other ancient towns, are irregularly formed, and several of them, it must be admitted, are inconveniently narrow. Many important alterations have however been made, under the provisions of an act obtained in 1821, for removing obstructions, watching, lighting, and the general improvement of the town, the powers of which are vested in trustees, who must be persons occupying property rated at £50 per annum to the street assessment, or worth £2000 above reprizes and resident within the town, or resident and receiving rents to the amount of £80 per annum, or non-resident and receiving rents from premises within the town worth £100 per annum, from whom a committee of management of nine individuals is selected, three of whom retire annually by rotation; and it has been remarked by one of the first members of this committee, " *that if judiciously chosen and faithful to their trust, our town may in time assume its due place among the cities of the empire.*"

In 1820 a company was established, with a capital of £8000, raised in 800 shares of £10 each, to supply the town with gas.

POPULATION.

The following official return of the population of the five parishes in Shrewsbury is according to the census ordered by government in 1831 :—

Parishes.	Houses.	Males.	Females.	Total.
St. Chad	1583	3496	4224	7720
St. Mary	1080	3087	3033	6120
St. Alkmond	356	820	958	1778
St. Julian	676	1413	1583	2996
Holy Cross & St. Giles	337	656	821	1477

Total population 20,091

ECCLESIASTICAL BUILDINGS.

The public structures devoted to the service of Religion are among the first objects that excite the attention, whilst by many they are not unfrequently looked upon with peculiar feelings of veneration and regard.

If the source of this feeling were traced, it would be found connected with those principles and associations which every one who acknowledges an all-bountiful Creator, or wishes well to his country, would desire to cherish.

Shrewsbury, we learn, did not receive much improvement from its original inhabitants, the Britons; yet what it lost in nominal consequence as the metropolis of a kingdom it ultimately gained in external splendour and real importance: this is evinced, among other proofs, by the erection of five ecclesiastical foundations, all of which were anterior to the Norman conquest, and originated in Saxon piety.

Among the earliest of these may be mentioned SAINT CHAD's, which is ascribed to one of the Mercian kings, who is said to have converted the palace of the kings of Powis into a church, about 780.

A dean and ten prebendaries or secular canons, with two vicars choral, under the patronage of the Bishop of Lichfield, are stated to have been placed here at a very remote period.

Under the Anglo-Saxon monarchs this college possessed twelve hides of arable land, or as much as paid for 1440 acres to what would be now called the land-tax; which, by proper cultivation, appears from the Survey of Domesday to have increased more than double. Other estates were subsequently added, which form now only insulated districts of the parish.

By the act of 1 Edward VI. 1547, the College was dissolved, the tythes and profits at that time being of the clear yearly value of about £50. The buildings and estates were leased out, reserving only the small stipend of £4. 6s. 8d. for the parish minister, charged on the dean's prebendal estate at Onslow.

Although a lease was granted of the tythes, yet only two years afterwards the greater portion of them were appropriated by Edward VI. in aid of the Free Grammar School.

In 1579 Queen Elizabeth granted the remaining possessions of the deanery to Sir Christopher Hatton; but the corporation and parish seem to have presented to the living from 1583 until 1658-9, from which time the patronage has rested with the crown.

SAINT ALKMUND's CHURCH owes its foundation to the piety of Ethelfleda, daughter of Alfred the Great, soon after she succeeded to the sovereignty of the Mercian territory in 912.

Her great nephew, King Edgar, being of the race of

the Northumbrian Prince Alkmund, increased the original endowment, and (under the direction of Archbishop Dunstan) appointed a dean and ten prebends.

In the reign of Edward the Confessor, this College possessed eleven manors, nine of which, containing upwards of 4000 acres) it retained at the Norman survey.

After experiencing many of the fluctuations common to property, sacred or otherwise, during the dark ages and under lawless government, these estates were at length alienated in 1147, at the particular request of the Dean, Richard de Belemis, and with the consent of King Stephen and Pope Eugenius III. to the monastery of Lilleshull, which the dean's brother, Philip de Belemis, had just commenced, the Prebendaries however taking care to reserve to themselves a life interest in their several stipends.

The college being thus early dissolved and deprived of its valuable estates, fell into a humble vicarage, which remained in the patronage of the monks of Lilleshull until the dissolution, when it lapsed to the crown, in whose hands it continued until 1628, when Rowland Heylin, Esq.* of Pentreheylin, Montgomeryshire, purchased the advowson for the " feoffees of St. Antholines," a society instituted for founding lectureships and augmenting small livings in populous towns.

This society having been publicly denounced, and the orthodoxy of its principles questioned, the ministers of King James, in 1663, directed its suppression, when the living again reverted to the crown.

* Mr. Heylin appears to have been connected with this town, having previously founded a lectureship in St. Alkmond's church, to which he afterwards added the tithe of Coton. In 1630 he was at the expence of printing the Welsh Bible in octavo, a form more suitable for domestic reading than the two former folio editions.

THE COLLEGIATE CHURCH OF ST. MARY is considered to have been founded by King Edgar, about the year 980; although, from the extensive limits of the parish, it is probable this was only the renovation of an older church destroyed by the ravages of the Danes, who, in revenging the slaughter of their predecessors, not only exercised their warfare against mankind, but even those works of ingenuity and labour which were consecrated to devotion did not escape their desolating hand.

In the time of Edward the Confessor, this college possessed an estate of nearly 1300 acres, " for the maintenance of a dean, seven prebendaries, and a parish priest," which appears to have diminished in point of cultivation and consequent value at the survey of Domesday, in which, however, the " vill of Chorleton," held in conjunction with the church of St. Juliana, is unnoticed, having probably been acquired afterwards.

At the suppression of colleges the revenue was £42, when Edward VI. appropriated the greater part of the tithes of this, as he had done those of St. Chad's parish, to the bailiffs and burgesses, for the foundation of a free school.

This church from very remote times has been a "royal free chapel," and thereby exempt from the jurisdiction of the bishop.

THE CHURCH OF ST. JULIANA.—Little is known of this, further than its origin was Saxon, and that it held in the Norman survey " half a hide of land in the city." Soon after this period it became distinguished as a rectory and royal free chapel, and was early united to the church of St. Michael within the Castle, now destroyed.*

* The site of St. Michael's church cannot be satisfactorily stated. Messrs. Owen and Blakeway consider that Speed's map represents it as standing near the river opposite the area of the present county gaol; but this must be a

In 1410, Henry IV. annexed both of these churches to his college at Battlefield; and being thus deprived of its property, St. Julian's became no better than a curacy.

THE CHURCH OF ST. PETER, called "*The Parish of the City*," was a small structure of wood, built about Edward the Confessor's time, by Siward, a Saxon nobleman, and stood on the site where Earl Roger de Montgomery founded a large Benedictine Abbey in 1083, which was re-dedicated to St. Peter, and endowed with a small portion of the vast possessions granted by the Conqueror to the first Earl of Shrewsbury.

This venerable warrior being seized with illness while residing in the castle he had lately built here,—apprehensive, too, that his dissolution might not be far distant,—and " to be sure of paradise,"—determined, with the consent of his countess Adelissa, to retire from the world, and become a monk within the confines of his own monastery.

This resolution he acted upon July 14th, 1094 : and dying three days afterwards, obtained honourable interment in the " Lady Chapel" of that pile he had zealously commenced, and,

" By skill of earthly architect,"

nearly completed, to the service and honour of his Maker.

Hugh, his second son, surnamed Probus for his courage, and Goch (or the Red) by the Welshmen from his com-

D

mistake, for Speed intended to shew the bastion tower of the castle. The chu·ch being probably only a very small structure, and designed by its founder (Roger de Montgomery) as a place of worship for those who inhabited the keep, it doubtless stood, as its name implies, WITHIN the walls (similar to the one at Ludlow Castle), and was taken down about 1605, before Speed's map was published. The present detached part of St. Julian's parish in the direction of Castle Foregate formed its parochial boundary.

plexion, succeeded to the earldom, and in filial affection came with his barons to the abbey, to visit his father's tomb; when he confirmed all former endowments, and gave many additional privileges, to which several of his barons added estates.*

Scarcely a century had elapsed from its foundation, before the monastery possessed " seventy-one distinct grants of manors or lands, twenty-four churches, the tithes of thirty-seven parishes or vills," besides many extensive immunities of various descriptions, and an almost matchless collection of unique relics, in addition to the remains of that popular " martyr," St. Wenefreda, which the monks procured, after many tedious negociations, from the priests and inhabitants of Gwytherin, in the county of Denbigh, in order to increase the celebrity of their house. After their translation hither, they were enshrined with much pomp near the high altar, and attracted multitudes of pilgrims, whose benefactions greatly contributed to the emolument of the church.

The abbot of this monastery had the honour of a seat in Parliament, and the authority of a bishop within his house. Of the 608 monasteries that existed in this kingdom at the time of the dissolution, it is recorded " the Abbey of Shrewsbury was 34th in opulence."

According to the valor of 26th Henry VIII. the annual income was £572. 15s. 5d. a revenue considered equal to about £4750 of modern currency.

The surrender of this abbey took place 24th January, 1539-40, when the estates and buildings immediately passed into lay hands.

* Earl Hugh was slain by an arrow in Anglesea, in the month of July, 1098, and received sepulture seventeen days after in the cloisters of this abbey. Twenty years ago, a plain stone coffin was discovered near the south-west door of the present church, which probably enclosed his remains.

St. Giles's Church was built early in the reign of Henry I. for the service of a hospital of lepers, which stood at the west end of the present edifice.

It is supposed to have become parochial about the middle of the fifteenth century, on being united with the parish of Holy Cross within the monastery, the abbot and convent, no doubt, having previously possessed the patronage and appointment of master.

Subsequent to these, were erected three large conventual churches and eight smaller chapels, all of which shared the fate of the dissolution; and of their remains the ceaseless operations of time and the hand of man have spared but few traces.

Several chantries, altars, &c. were also maintained by private donations in these churches; and whether we consider the munificence, the piety, or the superstition which raised them, we must respect the fervency towards a good cause, and regret that so much zeal was blessed with such little knowedge of the truths which, under our reformed religion, we now so happily enjoy.

From this cursory view of the piety of our forefathers, it may be justly asserted, that in the present day there is no provincial town in the kingdom, considering its extent, where so much has been done to promote the cause of religion, and to give a suitable effect to buildings set apart for Divine Worship, as in Shrewsbury. Those individuals, therefore, whose taste and liberality have mainly contributed to the accomplishment of this praiseworthy object, are deserving of the best thanks of their cotemporaries; and to them posterity will owe a debt of admiring gratitude, in those pleasing feelings of awe which insensibly steal o'er the mind while contemplating the architectural beauties of temples dedicated to HIM, whose greatness as far exceeds the capacity of human thought as doth the immensity of space the smallest atom.

Our survey of these interesting buildings will commence, in chronological arrangement, with

THE OLD CHURCH OF ST. CHAD.

"In midst of towne fower Parish Churches are,
Full nere and close, together note that right:
For they doe seeme a true love knot to sight."

These quaint lines of our native poet Churchyard, with

the illustrative vignette, describe the situation which the spacious cruciform church of Old Saint Chad occupied on the southern eminence of the town.

The period of its early foundation has been already alluded to, and the nearly total destruction of the fabric was occasioned by workmen having very injudiciously commenced under-building (contrary to the advice of an experienced architect,) one of the pillars that supported the large central tower, which had shrunk considerably from graves having been carelessly made too close to its foundations. The slight vibration occasioned by the chimes proclaiming their matin tune at four o'clock, on July 9th, 1788, caused the decayed pillar to give way, when the ponderous tower rent asunder, and with the heavy peal of bells it contained, falling on the roofs of the nave and transepts, crushed those parts of the edifice into ruinous desolation, producing a scene of horrid confusion more easily to be imagined than described. The masons had a narrow but fortunate escape, and were only waiting at the adjoining house of the sexton for the keys of the church, to pursue their misdirected scheme of economy.

The event excited a great consternation in the town, and the exemplary vicar, the Rev. Thomas Stedman, addressed an affectionate pastoral letter to his parishioners on the improvement that should be made of so remarkable an interposition of Providence, which occurred at a time when not a single person was within the reach of any injury from it.

Before the church fell, apprehensions were entertained that some fatal consequences might follow, from the appearances of decay in different parts of the building; these fears, however, were comparatively slight, and no immediate danger expected. But after the event took place it was found that the shattered state of the edifice was such, that instead of exciting surprise that it should fall when it did, there were just grounds for amazement that it should have stood so long. Had the decayed state of the building been thoroughly understood before it gave way, the probable opinion would have been, that whenever the disaster happened, it would be at a time when the effects of it might have been dreadful to many ;—as when the greatest weight was in the galleries, or when the tower had been shaken by the motion of the bells. Only a month previous, 3000 persons, it is considered, were assembled in the church to witness the interment of an officer under military honours.

The old church was a majestic edifice, erected in the reign of Henry III. in the style when the round Norman arches were giving way to the beautiful lancet style. In 1393 the roofs and tower, with the wooden spire covered with lead, were destroyed by a calamitous fire, occasioned by the negligence of a plumber while repairing the leads. The damage being considerable, Richard II. granted to the inhabitants a remission of their fee-farm rent, and certain other taxes, towards the re-edification.

From the fragments of Saxon sculpture discovered in portions of the walls after the fall of the late fabric, the edifice which preceded it must have been considerably adorned.

The dawning light of the Reformation in Shrewsbury first beamed in this church in 1407, by William Thorpe, a priest and disciple of the doctrines promulgated by Wickliff. This Salopian reformer, in a sermon before the bailiffs on the third Sunday after Easter, boldly preached against the prevailing and favourite tenets of the Romish church; for his temerity he was thrown into the prison of the town, by command of the local authorities, where he remained about a month, and was afterwards removed to Lambeth for examination before the archbishop, the bailiffs preferring the charge of heresy and schism against him.

The conduct of Thorpe before his spiritual superior was decent and respectful, but at the same time he remained zealous in his vindication of scripture, and firm in support of that which he considered the truth,—thus intrepidly answering the archbishop, " I'll tell you at one word, I dare not from the dread of God submit unto you, notwithstanding the tenure and sentence that you have rehearsed to me." He was accordingly sent back to prison : his subsequent fate is nowhere recorded, but it is conjectured on good grounds he was liberated after the death of the archbishop, so that what Fox has asserted of his having died a martyr to hard usage is probably incorrect.

The exercise of the Protestant religion in this town also began in this church in 1573, under the direction of the Bishop of Lichfield and the Lord President of the Marches, as special commissioners from Queen Elizabeth.

The portion of the ruins now remaining stood south of the choir, and formed a chantry chapel dedicated to the Virgin Mary; after the Reformation it was called the Bishop's Chancel, from the circumstance of its being used at the visitations of the bishop and archdeacon. The two wide semi-circular arches (now walled up) separated it from the transepts and choir. On the outside north wall are three stone stalls having pointed arches, the concaves of which are groined; these originally adjoined the high altar, and formed the seats of the priest, deacon, and sub-deacon, during a part of the high mass. The east and south sides display two mullioned windows; one adjoining the newel staircase in the south-west pier, which once led to the belfry is of an earlier design than the rest, and was probably introduced when the building was repaired in 1496 ; the others have elegant trefoiled tracery, and were erected in

1571, when the chapel was nearly rebuilt by Humphrey Onslow, Esq. to the dilapidations of which he appears to have been liable by the lease granted to him of the deanery when the dissolution of the college was anticipated in 1542-3.

The interior has an oak panelled ceiling, and contains a few monumental tablets and hatchments, most of the ancient memorials having been removed on the fall of the church to other places.

This chapel is now used as a daily parochial school, and for reading the burial service connected with the spacious cemetery in which it stands.

Among the monuments is one to the memory of that excellent man, the Rev. JOB ORTON, V. D. M. who " being dead, yet speaketh," in the forcible discourses and truly admirable writings he has left behind. He was the friend and biographer of Doddridge, and died 16th July, 1783, aged 66. His remains were interred at his request in the grave of the Rev. J. Bryan, M. A. an ejected minister from this church.

A humble gravestone near the railway leading towards Belmont records the death of Capt. JOHN BENBOW, who was shot at the Castle, Oct. 16th, 1651, for his attachment to the cause of King Charles the Second.

Several members of ancient families and distinguished individuals connected with the town and county, received interment in this church. Among these may be mentioned those of CORBET, MYTTON, BURTON, OWEN, LYSTER, and IRELAND.

ROWLAND LEE, Bishop of Lichfield and Coventry, and Lord President of the Marches, was buried here. He died Jan. 27th, 1542-3, at the College, the residence of his brother, Sir George Lee, who was the last dean of the church.

THE NEW CHURCH OF SAINT CHAD

is erected on a beautiful site near the Quarry, and, considering the disadvantages of form which preclude the possibility of much architectural effect, it may be looked upon as an ornamental building.

The church is formed by the intersection of two circles, with a tower and portico attached; the smaller of the circles forming the grand staircase, and the larger one the body, chancel, and side staircases leading to the gallery. On each side of the tower is a square wing 24 feet by 19, appropriated for a vestry and robing room.

The exterior is divided into two stories, the lower one being rusticated, and the upper springing from a moulding displaying a continued Ionic entablature, supported by coupled pilasters of the same order; above the cornice is a well-proportioned balustrade.

The windows are circular headed in the upper, and square in the lower story, and, with the exception of that in the chancel, are uniform; the latter is Venetian, the divisions being formed with Corinthian pillars.

The portico consists of four Roman Doric columns and entablature in full order, and is considered a very fine specimen.

The steeple is divided into three parts, and, like the body of the church, is rusticated at the base, which is square; on this rests the second division, or bell chamber, octangular in shape, and decorated with Ionic pilasters, cornice, &c.; above rises eight elegant Corinthian columns, surrounded with an iron railing, and surmounted by a dome and cross.

THE INTERIOR carries with it an air of importance, grandeur, and extent, derived mainly from that form which in the exterior has so much shackled the efforts of the architect: dazzled for a moment by the first impressions, the detail is lost in the general effect; but from the whole the eye is directed to those parts which constitute that whole, and here defects may be discovered that will not stand the test of architectural scrutiny.

The seats are well constructed, every individual being able to see the officiating minister. The gallery is not thrown too forward, but is in every respect in unison with the size of the church; it is carried round the whole area with the exception of the chancel, and is supported by a double row of ill-proportioned Ionic columns, painted porphyry. A continued balustrade finishes the front of the gallery, from which rises slender fluted columns (surmounted with entablature) for the support of the roof, the frieze being decorated with cherubs.

The ceiling is enriched with a glory and cherubs in the centre, surrounded by a wreath and other devices.

The chancel, contrary to general custom, is towards the north, and is separated from the body of the church by a handsome arch springing from an entablature supported by coupled composite columns, elegantly proportioned, the capitals of which are richly gilt.

The altar-piece is plain oak wainscot, with panels inscribed according to the canon of the church, above which is a Venetian window, containing a painting in enamelled glass of the Resurrection of our Saviour, by the elder Eginton. This window is shortly to be replaced by another, our townsman, Mr. David Evans, having been directed by the munificence of the Rev. Richard Scott, B.D. to exert his talents in the execution of a splendid and faithful copy of the celebrated chef d'ouvre of Rubens, painted for the cathedral church of Antwerp, THE DESCENT FROM THE CROSS, with the VISITATION, and PRESENTATION IN THE TEMPLE.

The pulpit and reading desk stand in the centre of the area in front of the chancel.

The organ is placed above the south or great entrance of the church; it is in a mahogany case, with a small painting of David playing upon the harp. The instrument was built by Gray, of London, and cost 400 guineas.

Between the piers of the gallery-windows are hatchments; and the building, although of modern date, contains several tasteful memorials which indicate,

> " All that virtue, all that wealth e'er gave,
> Await alike the inevitable hour—
> The paths of glory lead but to the grave."

Among these may be mentioned a large panelled tablet, having a bust of the deceased by Chantrey, within a recess, commemorative of Mr. John Simpson, "who superintended the building of this church; the bridges of Bewdley, Dunkeld, Craig, Ellachie, and Bonar; the aqueducts of Pontcysyllte and Chirk; and the locks and basins of the Caledonian Canal." He died 1815.

On each side of the entrance leading to the chancel are tablets, highly enriched with sculpture, recording the decease of the Rev. George Scott, of Betton Strange, in this parish, and of Ann Lucretia, his wife; also of Richard Scott, of Peniarth Ucha, Merionethshire, and Underdale, in the county of Salop.

On the east wall of the chancel is a small tablet in memory of

The Rev. THOMAS STEDMAN, M. A.
" Forty-two years Vicar of this Parish, during which period
his mind, his writings, and his discourse
were with deep humility devoted
to the glory of God, the happiness of mankind,
and the temporal and spiritual interests of his flock."
He died Dec. 5th, 1825, in the 80th year of his age.

On a large Grecian tablet is a Latin inscription to the memory of the late Rev. Francis Leighton, M. A. who died Sept. 7th, 1813, aged 66 years.*

The body of the church is 100 feet in diameter, and the total length, including the entrance and vestibule, 160 feet. The building is of fine Grinshill stone, and was designed by Mr. George Steuart, of London. It was com-

---

* He was a gentleman of warm piety and extensive benevolence; as a scholar and linguist he was scarcely surpassed by any of his contemporaries. He meditated a History of Shropshire, which, had it been completed, it is probable the world would have seen, from his diffusive acquirements and general antiquarian knowledge, a very superior topographical work.

menced March 2d, 1790, and consecrated August 20th, 1792, and will comfortably accommodate a congregation of about 2300 persons. The total cost, including site, organ, bells, &c. was £19,352, of which £15,800 was raised under act of parliament.

The steeple is 150 feet in height, and contains a full and melodious peal of twelve bells; the weight of the tenor being 2 tons 1 cwt. and measures 16 ft. 6 in. in circumference at the mouth. The balcony beneath the dome commands a fine prospect of the town and immediate vicinity.

In the vestry is a carved statue of St. Chad in his episcopal habit, holding a bible in his right hand and a crosier in his left. It originally stood upon the organ in the old church.

St. Chad's is considered the principal church of the town; it is used on all public occasions, and is the place where the archdeacon holds his visitations and probat court.

A lecture is delivered here every Thursday evening, according to a bequest of the late James Phillips, Esq. of London, who by his will (dated 1661) devises, after the death of his wife, the rents of his property in Three Crown Court, Southwark, unto the mayor and aldermen of this town for that purpose, and also for a lecture in the parish churches of Oswestry, Ellesmere, and Whitchurch. This property now produces a good revenue.

On the east side of the church is a spacious cemetery.

The living is a vicarage in the gift of the crown, being endowed in 1674, by the benefaction of Nathaniel Tench, Esq. with " the tithes of corn and hay of the grange of Crow Meole," in commemoration of which the testator directed that a sermon should be annually preached on the 6th of June.

The parish comprises nearly one-half of the town, and

E

extends several miles into the country, having two chapels of ease,—St. George's (Frankwell), and Bicton, three miles distant.

ST. MARY'S CHURCH

stands on a commanding situation, nearly one hundred feet above the level of the river, on the north-eastern side of the town, and is one of the most interesting ecclesiastical edifices in the county, displaying in its construction almost every variety of ancient architecture, and affording to the antiquary and man of taste a rich and unique field for observation.

It is a cruciform building, consisting of a nave, side aisles, transepts, spacious chancel, two chantry chapels, and a lofty spire steeple.

In common with our early churches we have no opportunity of ascertaining the precise date of its erection on written testimony. The probable period of foundation has been stated, page 24 ; the renovation and subsequent addition is therefore presumptive, and our decision must be governed by analogy of style with other edifices, whose origin is authenticated.

That the era of ancient buildings may be inferred from the internal evidence they themselves afford of their respective antiquity admits of little doubt ; indeed, the amiable poet, Gray, who had much knowledge in antiquarian pursuits, has said that " they constantly furnish, to the well informed eye, arms, ornaments, and other indubitable marks by which their several ages may be ascertained."

There will be little difficulty in appropriating the ancient portions of this building to distinct ages, if we except the task of assigning a correct criteria to the curious mixture displayed in the columns which support the semicircular arches of the nave, where the Norman and pointed styles are singularly blended together, the union of which will afford matter of interesting speculation to the experienced antiquary.

William of Malmesbury has related an anecdote of the pious Wolstan, Bishop of Worcester (from 1062 to 1095) praying, on his way to Chester, in the *wooden church of St. Peter*, in this town,* and of the " citizens

* Page 25.

asking him why he preferred it to the church which they called St. Mary's ;"—a question we may reasonably conclude as shewing this was then, in their opinion, from some circumstance, a church of no little consequence.

The superior taste and enlarged views of improvement manifested by the Normans in the arts, caused the restoration of many important churches in much less time than a century after they had obtained the conquest of our island.

St. Mary's, no doubt, from its antiquity, required restoration, and excited their early attention; but although destitute of positive data, as before stated, from whence to ascribe a period to its re-edification, the various improvements plainly evident in several parts of the fabric will easily be discovered by the critical eye of the architectural antiquary.

It may be mentioned that three distinct styles are apparent,—the Anglo-Norman of the 12th century, in the basement of the tower, nave, transepts, and doorways; the early lancet style in the windows of the transepts and chancel; the pointed and obtuse arch of the 15th and 16th century in the side aisles, clere-story, chantry, chapels, &c.

These shall be carefully examined by analysis, and the predominant features appropriated with caution to their respective periods.

The greater part of a new structure, it is therefore conjectured, was raised on the site of a previous Saxon building, probably early in the reign of Henry I. This is evident from the plain circular windows inserted in the massive basement of the tower, which, like the lower portion of the entire building, is of red stone, and flanked by broad flat buttresses, similar to those on the lower part of the Abbey tower.

The tower of St. Mary's originally was probably not higher than the part composed of red stone, and was terminated like the generality of Norman towers, by a plain parapet.

The struggle between the Norman and pointed styles sometimes occasioned incongruous arches, and we may attribute the rude pointed doorway of the tower having an internal arch nearly triangular, to the reign of Stephen.

THE SOUTH PORCH of the nave is of the early Norman era, the outward arch circular, having zigzag mouldings issuing from clustered columns, and an inner rib, obtusely pointed ; the windows on each side are curious as early specimens of the rudiments of the mullioned window, introduced about the time of Stephen ; the arches of these windows rest on short thick columns, and are bisected into two lights by a similar pillar as a mullion, the capitals of which are all different ; in the apex is a quatrefoil, one of the simplest and most ancient kind of ornaments.

The ceiling of the porch is also an example of the most ancient kind of groined vault, having neither boss nor ornament ; above this is a chamber (entered from the church by a newel staircase), and lighted by a pointed window.

The inner doorway of the porch is an enriched round arch, with chevron, lozenge, and foliated mouldings. That on the north side of the nave is similar in style ; and the doorways (now closed) in the north and south transepts are very elegant specimens of the style which prevailed from the Conquest to the time of Henry I. ; the latter is decorated with alternate lozenge panels filled with an embossed flower.

A progressive movement of refinement and beauty took place in the science of architecture during the reign of Henry III. when the heavy Norman was succeeded by the slender lancet arch and its attendant ornaments. The transepts of this church are fine specimens of this transition of the styles, the north and south ends of which are terminated by beautifully proportioned triple lancet windows enriched with slender shafts and mouldings.

About the close of the 15th century, a greater stateliness of character and ornamental arrangement became the prevailing characteristic of architectural display, and the general features of the building were altered to the fashionable style.

The walls of the side aisles previous to this time were much lower, which is indicated by a slope in the stone work at the west end and a pier at the south-west, on which the roof originally rested. When the walls were raised, three mullioned windows were substituted on each side for round-headed lights, which narrowed towards the exterior surface of the wall, similar, no doubt, to that still remaining at the west end.

The nave shortly afterwards received the addition of a clere-story, lighted by a range of short windows with obtusely pointed arches, extending the whole length of the nave and chancel.

To render these important alterations of the fabric complete, the low massy tower was raised, and large double pointed windows were placed on each side, and the whole surmounted with an embattled parapet and pinnacles, which (being much decayed) were judiciously restored in 1816. From this tower rises an octagonal spire of noble proportions, which may be ranked as equal in height to the *third loftiest spire* in the kingdom, and forms an interesting and prominent object from every part of the rich and beautiful scenery which surrounds the town.

The dimensions, as taken at the last repair in 1818, are—tower, 78 feet 4 inches ; spire, to the top of vane, 141 feet 10 inches ; total height, 220 feet 2 inches.

The chapel south of the chancel has a remarkably lofty roof, and on the south side four handsome pointed windows of Henry the Sixth's time ; each window is divided by a buttress, on which rests a crocketed pinnacle. The eastern end of this building was originally finished by a large window, but within its space two lofty round-headed lights, with singular canopies in the debased style, prevalent about the reign of Queen Elizabeth, have been inserted.

The chancel is terminated by a large window, divided by mullions into two tiers of eight lights each, the apex being ramified into inelegant tracery, introduced in repairing the damage which this window (and that alluded to in the above chapel) sustained during an extreme tempest in 1579.

THE INTERIOR

of this church is strikingly noble, and calculated to inspire the mind with awe ; but although the purer light of later times has in some degree eclipsed the adventitious aid intended to be conveyed to the feelings, during the religious ceremonies of our forefathers, by the almost mysterious effect produced from intermingled arches and clustered columns, canopied niches, costly shrines, and the mellow reflection of the storied pane shedding

"The dim blaze of radiance richly clear,"

in these august edifices of former ages, they still possess a power over the imagination, and insensible must that mind be which is not susceptible of appropriate religious influences,—subdued thoughts,—and inspiring conceptions of divine majesty, when beholding the " long drawn aisle" and " high embower'd roof," where all forms and differences of opinion, it has been justly remarked, become " trivial for awhile, amidst the sublimity of temples so well suited to the adoration of omnipotence."

The nave is separated from the side aisles by *four*

semicircular arches, resting on elegant clustered columns, with capitals decorated with foliage of different devices, from the rudest to the richest design. The mouldings of these arches have bolder projections, but are less massive than those of the early Norman, and more delicately finished, and although the mouldings on the shafts are peculiar to the earliest pointed style, they happily harmonize with the circular arches.

At the eastern extremity of each side aisle, opening to the transepts, is a semi-circular arch, resting on thick round pillars, with a regular base and indented capital, ornamented with sculpture of the earliest Norman era; similar arches lead to the chantry chapels. These arches, from their general style, are evidently the oldest part of the fabric, and we may venture to ascribe them to a period not later than the Conquest. In removing the accumulations of colouring and plaister from the walls and arches of this part, in 1828, the *distinguishing marks* of the *operative masons* employed in working the stones were discovered, and still are to be seen, being the same as those now used.*

The choir and transepts are divided by three most beautiful pointed arches, rising from piers similar to those described in the nave.

The ceiling of the nave is of oak, the intersections of the beams being formed into panels richly decorated with ornamented quatrefoils and foliage, carved bosses, flowers, grotesque figures, &c. A beautiful cornice of vine branches, grapes interspersed with masks, are placed round the walls beneath the roof. The whole is in excellent

* About the close of the 12th century, companies of masons, designers, or architects, as well as workmen, were incorporated under the especial patronage of the Pope, and associated together as a fraternity of free and accepted masons, under certain regulations and peculiar privileges.

preservation, and supposed to be one of the finest specimens of the ancient fretted ceiling in the kingdom.

THE CHANCEL is elevated above the church by a double ascent, and the ceiling, like that of both the transepts, is excellently painted, but panelled in a style somewhat similar to that of the nave, and adorned with some of the rich fret work removed from the wreck of the churches of St. Chad and St. Alkmond.

On the north side of the altar is a most beautiful triple lancet window, with arches remarkably acute, and resting on isolated columns, whose capitals are adorned with elegant foliage, &c. The window is filled with three figures in ancient stained glass.

Whilst these pages are passing through the press, a most important improvement has been effected in the chancel, by removing the altar screen, which, although a handsome Grecian design, obstructed not only much of the eastern window, but was quite out of character with the building. Another of a more appropriate description will be substituted.

The eastern window contains the truly splendid glass that adorned the chancel of old St. Chad's, and which escaped the destruction that befel the other parts of the fabric. It was carefully removed and presented to this parish by the trustees for putting into execution the act for rebuilding the new church.

This glass, unequalled in point of beauty and colouring, represents THE GENEALOGY OF CHRIST, from the root of Jesse. The patriarch occupies the breadth of three bays of the window, being depicted as reclining in a deep sleep, with his head resting upon an embroidered pillow, and supported on his right hand. From his loins issues a VINE, the branches of which, before its disarrangement, overspread the whole window, inclosing within the ovals formed by its intersections a KING or PROPHET of the ancestry of Joseph, the series of which is finished by the husband of the Virgin Mary in a devotional posture at the feet of his progenitor.

Many of the figures are depicted with their peculiar emblems. The ground of the whole is varied and exquisitely vivid, on which the clusters of grapes and the bright verdure of the vine leaves are displayed with great effect.

Two compartments contain figures of ancient knights vested in the hawberk and bearing their square banners, and kneeling beneath foliated tabernacles. They represent Sir John Cherleton, Lord of Powis, and his son Sir Owen. From the following translation of an inscription on a part of the window,

" Pray for Monsieur John de Charlton, who caused this glazing to be made, and for Dame Hawis his companion,"

the date of its erection is ascertained to be about the middle of the fourteenth century; it was originally placed in the church of the convent of Grey Friars in this town, from whence it was removed to St. Chad's at the Dissolution.

Many of the figures have been displaced in their change of situation; their re-arrangement, however, is now in progress, and to complete the genealogical line additional figures will be added, and the lower tier of arches in the window, formerly filled with brick-work, have been opened to their base.

At the west end of the nave is a peculiarly rich and full-toned organ, made by the celebrated builders Harris and Byfield, in 1729, which has recently been improved by the addition of an octave and a half of pedal pipes.

This instrument stands upon a handsome stone screen, divided into three compartments, formed by as many obtusely pointed arches, and divided by buttresses of two stories, highly decorated with reticulated divisions, containing an open flower in relief: around the inner recesses of the arches are the following inscriptions:—

Uenite Domino exultemus
Rupi salutis jubilemus
Iehovam hymnis concinamus
Et grates illi persolvamus—Hallelujah.

Iehovam virgines laudate
Senes et pueri celebrate
Psalmis ecclesia sanctorum
Extollat Dominum Dominorum.

Laudate carminis clamore
Laudate buccinae clangore
Laudate organo sonoro
Laudate cymbalis et choro.

Above is a series of smaller arches similar in style, having cinque-foil heads, and filled with the like reticulated divisions and ornament, each of the arches being divided by a small plain buttress; the string course is charged with elaborately carved heads of angels, pateras, &c. and the spandrils of the several arches throughout are enriched with elegant and varied foliage, exquisitely sculptured. The whole forming a most prominent and imposing feature to the main entrance of the nave, and will be a permanent monument of the good taste and munificence of the donor, the Rev. W. G. Rowland, M. A.

The screen was designed by and executed under the superintendence of Mr. John Carline, of this town, and is a work creditable to his professional abilities.

THE NORTH TRANSEPT

has a rich and pleasing appearance on entering the church

from the eastern door,* through a porch which was once a chantry chapel, and connected with the transept by a fine Norman arch.

The triple windows of this and the corresponding transept are filled with small full-length figures in stained glass, bearing their respective insignia, and judiciously placed within ovals of chaste mosaic patterns. The centre of the middle light has the arms of King George the Third, with the following inscription:

GEO. III.
REGUM · OPTIMUS ·
GENTIS · BRITANNICAE ·
OLIM · DELICIÆ · NUNC · DESIDERIUM ·
MORTALITATEM · EXUIT ·
MENS · JAN · DIE · 29 · A · D. 1820 ·
ANNO · ÆTAT · 82 . REGNI · 60 .

On a scroll at the top,
Among many Nations was there no King like him.—Neh. xiii. 26.

On another at the bottom,
His Heart was perfect with the Lord all his Days.—1 Kings xv. 14.

Above these arms is the figure of the Virgin Mary, and below is St. Andrew. The dexter lancet window is occupied with the figures of St. Philip, St. Bartholomew, and St. James the son of Zebedee, and the sinister with St. Simon, St. Thomas, and St. Matthias. At the bottom is the following inscription:—" IOANNES BRICKDALE BLAKEWAY, A. M. HUJUS ECCLESIÆ JUDEX OFFICIALIS ET MINISTER INSIGNIA REGIA P. C. ANNO MDCCCXX. RELIQUAM FENESTRÆ PARTEM EXORNAVIT EJUS VIDUA M. E. B. ANNO MDCCCXXIX.

The lower portion of the walls are ornamented with interstitial divisions and monuments.

---

* This is now a principal entrance to the church; the jambs of the door-way are in the debased style prevalent during the last century, and the obtuse arch seems originally to have formed the head of a window.

THE NORTH TRANSEPT.

Against the west wall is a most beautiful free-stone

𝔐onument

TO THE LATE REV. J. B. BLAKEWAY;

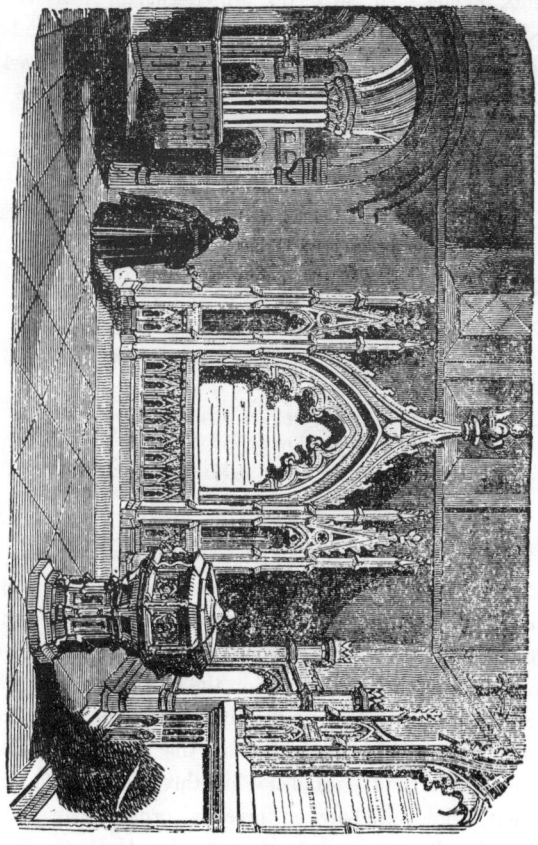

which for elegance of design, beauty of execution, and

F

general effect, has perhaps rarely been surpassed in modern times.

This beautiful Memorial was designed by Mr. John Carline, of this town, and is upwards of 12 feet in length and 16 feet in height, and is divided into three compartments by clustered buttresses, which sustain richly crocketed pinnacles. The centre compartment comprises a large pointed arch, cusped, canopied, and crocketed, the back of which is deeply recessed, and contains the following inscription in ornamental Roman capitals:

To the Memory of the Reverend
JOHN BRICKDALE BLAKEWAY, M. A. F. A. S
Thirty-one years Ordinary and Official
And Thirty-two years Minister of this Parish,
This Monument is erected
By the Voluntary Subscription of his Parishioners,
As a tribute of respect for his talents,
Esteem for his virtues,
And gratitude for his long and faithful services
As their Friend and Pastor.
He died the tenth day of March, MDCCCXXVI.
Aged sixty years.

On each side of the above compartment is an elegant niche with a cinquefoil head, octagonal back, and groined ceiling. These niches are surmounted by acute-angled crocketed canopies formed of deep mouldings; and resting on the head of each niche within the canopy is a cinquefoil within a circle. In a similar situation in the centre compartment is a shield containing the following arms:—
Argent, on a bend engrailed sable, three bezants; impaling argent, a fess vaire between three unicorns passant, gules.

The above divisions rest on an altar tomb, the front of which is divided into twelve small niches with trefoil heads.

These niches are separated by small buttresses, with crocketed canopies and pinnacles.

Mr. Blakeway was the son of Joshua Blakeway, Esq. of this town, and a gentleman whose pleasing adaptation of manners and amiable walk through life gained him the universal respect of his fellow townsmen. Neither the church nor the state had a more faithful defender of its rights or supporter of its dignity, nor the true interests of his native town a more watchful guardian.

As a scholar and a gentleman, united with the character of a true christian, we shall perhaps " ne'er look upon his like again." As a preacher he was admired for his forcible illustration of holy writ, and the valuable admonitions clothed in the language of affection which his discourses generally contained, whilst his devoutness in the performance of the sacred duties of the sanctuary must have impressed their importance on all who heard them. In his personal appearance he was tall and robust;—his face bore the line of thought, and his ample forehead bespoke the mind that dwelt within. As an author he had written much and published little, and was known only to the literary world previous to 1821 by a few sermons, controversial tracts, and critical notes in Malone's edition of Boswell's Life of Johnson. His name, however, will be immortalized in the valuable History of Shrewsbury which he commenced in 1820, with the Venerable Archdeacon Owen, and just lived to see the general history and ecclesiastical portions published in two quarto volumes, which elaborate undertaking will obtain for him and his revered friend and colleague the respect and gratitude of every true Salopian in subsequent generations.

Mr. Blakeway likewise shewed much attention and devotedness to the antiquities of his native county, and the valuable mass of manuscripts he left behind in illustration of its genealogical and topographical history will remain also as a monument of his industry.*

His last end was peace,—for he departed almost without a sigh, and nearly without losing that benignant smile which was so peculiar to him. His remains were interred on the right of the west entrance to the church-yard.

Three beautiful specimens of monumental sculpture, designed by the same architect, occupy the north wall, and harmonize with the splendid memorial just described, a detail of which would occupy too much space. The lancet window in the west wall contains a fine ancient figure in stained glass of St. John the Evangelist, arrayed in a robe which displays a most splendid specimen of the ancient ruby glass of the old masters: the hem of the garment is brilliantly studded with pearls.

THE ANCIENT FONT stands in the centre of the area, and is very handsome. The basin is octangular, each side having an ornamented quatrefoil, in the centre of which is a large double rose. The angles have been adorned with busts of angels bearing shields, and the pedestal is pierced into gothic arches, divided by small shelving buttresses.

In the north-eastern angle is an octangular turret, in which a small doorway opens to a staircase leading to a chamber which was no doubt once a chantry. It is lighted by a curious triangular window, with a trefoil on the intrado

* In 1831 was published Mr. Blakeway's SHERIFFS OF SHROPSHIRE, illustrated with their armorial bearings, and notices genealogical and biographical of their families, edited with great judgment by a reverend gentleman of this town, a particular friend of the deceased. It is perhaps the first work in which what may be termed the genealogy and biography of a county has been distinctly treated, and evinces in a high degree the patient and diligent research of its talented author, whose valuable life we have reason to deplore was not spared to publish a History of the County of Salop, for which his talents and extensive local knowledge rendered him so eminently qualified.

of each arch, the mouldings of which are deeply recessed. Below this is another chantry chapel, now used as a VESTRY, having at the east end an early Norman light, and on the north a mullioned window of the fifteenth century. Under a low pointed arch beneath this window is a monumental tomb composed of alabaster, but sunk into the floor for economy of space: it bears the figures of a warrior and his lady in the act of devotion, supposed to represent Nicholas Stafford and his wife Katherine. The former was bailiff of the town in 1458, and died in 1471.

SOUTH TRANSEPT.

The window of this transept contains the figures of our Saviour, St. James the son of Alpheus, and St. Thaddeus; in the dexter compartments are those of St. Matthew the Evangelist, St. Paul, and St. Mark; and in the sinister those of St. John the Evangelist, St. Peter, and St. Luke. Underneath this window is "GULIELMUS GORSUCH ROWLAND A. M. HUJUS ECCLESIÆ JUDEX OFFICIALIS ET MINISTER HANC FENESTRAM FACIENDAM CURAVIT ANNO 1829.

The windows of this and the north transept were executed by Mr. D. Evans, of Shrewsbury, and may be considered as some of the finest specimens of the art in the kingdom, both as regards brilliancy and harmony of colours, beauty of design, and exquisite workmanship, whilst the " dim religious light" which they shed around, imparts an impressiveness of character that at once bespeaks the sacred purpose of the place as the House of Prayer.

Below the south window of this transept is a bold composition of monumental architecture, designed by Mr. J. Carline, consisting of three acute-angled crocketed canopies, crowned with a finial.   The labels of the arches are enriched with foliage, and the interior sweep fashioned in the ogee manner. From the lateral piers, and between each division of the arches, springs an elegant crocketted pinnacle panelled and finished by an open flower.

It is much to be wished that the correct taste displayed in these and other beautiful specimens of the decorated style of monumental architecture, recently erected in this church, was more generally manifested in the adaptation of monuments to the character of the buildings in which they are to be placed, instead of the unsightly tablets so commonly introduced, and which frequently contribute anything but ornament to our ancient churches.

From the south transept a fine Norman arch opens to the

TRINITY CHAPEL,

which also has a communication with the chancel by an arch in the pointed style.

This building (57 feet by 30) was at first of smaller dimensions, as is evident from two lancet windows (beneath which are two very early loop holes) in the wall next to the south aisle. Immediately above the shelving portion still visible of the roof of the original chapel is a peculiar circular window.

The enlargement was effected by the Draper's Company soon after their incorporation in 1461, having therein a guild or fraternity to the Holy Trinity. Within the south wall is the sedilia formerly used by the officiating priests, and the remains of a piscina, all of which were once overspread with elegant canopies.

On the opposite side is a large pointed arch, now walled up. Under this is an altar tomb, the sides of which are divided by small buttresses in ornamental niches of the early decorated style. Above is a mutilated recumbent figure of a cross-legged knight in linked armour, supposed to represent one of the LEYBURNES LORDS OF BERWICK, in this parish, and who died about the middle of the 14th century. The grave below was opened in 1816, and was composed of wrought masonry, when, after a little loose rubbish had been removed, some leg and thigh bones were discovered. On digging about three feet lower to the bottom of the tomb, a skeleton was found wrapped in leather, but without a head. This is conjectured to be the skeleton of Thomas Percy, Earl of Worcester, who was beheaded after the battle of Shrewsbury, and his head sent to London, while his body found an asylum in the tomb of a family which had become extinct.

This church, in 1232, was the scene of an assemblage of legates, convened by command of the Pope to hear charges which had been preferred against Llewelyn for repeated infractions of treaties. This negociation was at length left to six referees on the part of King Henry III. and four on that of the Welsh Prince, by which peace was maintained for a season.

When Charles the First visited this town in 1642, it is recorded he took " a protestation and the sacrament upon it to defend the Protestant religion established by Queen Elizabeth and his royal father," which solemn scene, it is supposed, took place within this edifice, being the parish church of the mansion in which he was sojourning. King James the Second, it is also said, attended divine service here in 1687, after which he exercised the royal gift of healing by touching many persons for the king's evil.

THE MONUMENTS of particular interest having been already noticed in their proper situations, it need only be remarked that there are mural tablets commemorative of individuals connected with the families of LYSTER, LLOYD (of Rûg, &c.), MORHALL, BLAKEWAY, &c. on the walls of the chancel, and several other memorials in the nave, transepts, and chapel; which the extended description of this church, and the confined limits of the present work, will not permit further to enumerate.

The length of the building from east to west is 160 feet, breadth (including side aisles) 50 feet.

The tower contains a peal of ten bells, the harmony of which, it is considered, cannot be excelled by that of any peal in the kingdom: weight of tenor 21 cwt. 2 qrs. 17 lbs.

On the west wall of the steeple is an inscription to the memory of Thomas Cadman, who lost his life in a bold attempt to descend from the top of the spire by means of a rope, which he had fixed to it and brought down to the Gay meadow, on the other side of the river Severn. He fell near the Water-lane gate, Feb. 2, 1739, aged 28, at a time when " the ground was iron and the Severn glass," owing, as the epitaph records, to

"A faulty cord being drawn too tight."

The parish of Saint Mary extends several miles in detached parts of the country, having within its boundaries five chapels of ease, viz. Albrighton, Astley, Berwick, Clive, and St. Michael's (Castle-foregate).

The church is a royal peculiar, and the official court has probate of all wills and cognizance of all other ecclesiastical matters arising within the parish. The living is a perpetual curacy, and was, previous to the late municipal act, in the presentation of the Corporation of Shrewsbury; and in the choice of a minister, the son of a burgess, who has been educated at the royal free grammar school, or (in case there be no burgess's son of that description) one born in the parish of Chirbury, with a qualification similar to the foregoing, is to have the preference.

SAINT ALKMUND'S CHURCH

is situate at a short distance from St. Mary's, and its cemetery adjoins that of St. Julian's.

The fine old cruciform church of this parish was inconsiderately destroyed in 1794, under a mistaken apprehension of its stability. The present building, with the exception of the tower and spire, which fortunately escaped the fate of the old church, was opened for divine service Nov. 8, 1795, at a cost of rather more than £3000.

The new structure is of Grinshill stone, and in the style called modern gothic, having six lofty pointed windows on each side, filled with slender mullions of cast-iron; between the windows are graduated buttresses.

The interior is handsomely fitted up, and the general effect pleasing, although not in strict conformity with a gothic building,—wanting that sombre grandeur characteristic of this style of architecture. It is 82 feet long by 44 feet wide, with a small chancel terminated by a pointed window filled with enamelled glass emblematical of " EVANGELICAL FAITH," depicted in the character of a female figure in the attitude of kneeling upon a cross, with her arms extended, and eyes elevated towards a celestial crown which appears in the opening clouds. The countenance has an interesting expression of adoration, and the motto, " Be thou faithful unto death," &c. is inscribed on an open volume. The window was painted by the elder Egginton, and cost 200 guineas,

At the west end is a capacious gallery, containing a small fine-toned organ by Gray, of London, erected by a subscription in 1823.

The principal entrance to the church is in the base of the tower, under an elegant pointed arch recessed within a square aperture, on either side of which are niches, most barbarously repaired in 1825; above is a bold mullioned window in the style of the sixteenth century, when the tower and spire were probably built. In this window are two ancient escutcheons in stained glass, displaying England and France quarterly, and the arms of Richard Sampson, Bishop of Lichfield, and Lord President of the Marches from 1543 to 1548.

The tower is finely proportioned, being flanked with double buttresses gradually diminishing, and terminated with a crocketted pinnacle; an open parapet of pointed arches surmounts the base of the spire, which, though not remarkable for height, is considered by persons of good taste " to possess singular elegance of form." The tower contains eight musical bells, recast in 1813, and is 70 feet high, the spire 114, making a total of 184 feet from the ground.

In a vault beneath this church are interred the remains of Thomas Jones, Esq. who died in 1642. He was six times bailiff, and the FIRST MAYOR OF SHREWSBURY; also those of Sir Thomas Jones, Lord Chief Justice of the Court of Common Pleas, who died 1692, to whom and other members of this ancient Shropshire family are several memorials. Other monumental tablets also relieve the walls of the building.

The old structure contained many curious brasses and monuments; the former were sold, and the latter dispersed, on its unnecessary demolition.

The living is a vicarage in the gift of the Crown, and a weekly lecture is preached in the church on Wednesdays.

SAINT JULIAN'S CHURCH.

The church, dedicated to St. Juliana, occupies an elevated situation at the top of Wyle Cop, and was erected 1749-50, from a design by Mr. T. F. Prichard, of this town, on the site of an Anglo-Norman structure, which had become ruinous.

It is a plain oblong building of brick, and stone dressings, 83 feet by 48, with a small recess for the chancel.

At the west end is the tower of the old church; the

basement is of red stone, and of a date far anterior to the superstructure, which is of the 16th century, and crowned by a handsome embattled parapet and eight lofty pinnacles, restored in 1818, when the masonry of the tower was chipped and repaired. The tower contains a peal of six bells, recast in 1706, and an excellent clock, the dial of which is illuminated at night.

In the south wall of the chancel is an ancient figure, probably intended to represent St. Juliana.

The interior is particularly neat, possessing an air of solemnity unusual in the generality of modern churches. Four large Roman-Doric pillars support the roof of the nave, which is carved and adorned with the fret-work of the old church. Galleries occupy three sides of the building. At the west end is an excellent organ, by Bowsher and Fleetwood, of Liverpool, erected by a subscription in 1834, the exterior of which is tasteful in design, and harmonizes with the internal architecture of the edifice.

The pulpit is handsome, and belonged to the old church. The altar-piece and furniture of the chancel are in good taste; the former is of wainscot, and presents a Roman Doric basement, supporting Ionic pilasters and entablature with modillion cornice, from which springs a rich architrave surrounding a Venetian window, in the centre light of which is a figure in stained glass of St. James bearing the Holy Scriptures. The side lights contain the royal arms, and those of the see of Lichfield, impaling Cornwallis.

In the windows of the south gallery are the armorial bearings of Queen Elizabeth, the family of Bowdler, a fine ancient shield of the town arms, and heads of St. Peter and St. Paul, surmounted by their emblems, the keys and sword. On the north side are the arms of Prince, Bennett, Astley, the Earl of Tankerville, and a figure of St. John.

In the floor of the south aisle is an ancient gravestone,

preserved from the former church: round the edge is a Longobardic inscription to the memory of Edmund Tromwyn, who is supposed to have died about the close of the thirteenth century.

There are several mural monuments in the aisles and chancel: on the north side of the latter is a pedimented tablet set on a square table of dove-coloured marble, with the following inscription :—

Sacred to the Memory
Of the VENERABLE HUGH OWEN, M.A. F.R.S.
Archdeacon of Salop,
Prebendary of Salisbury and Lichfield,
One of the Portionists of Bampton, Oxfordshire,
Formerly Minister of this Parish, and afterwards of St. Mary, in
Shrewsbury.
He was the only son of Pryce Owen, M.D. and Bridget his wife,
And the lineal descendant of an Ancient British family.
Distinguished for the extent and accuracy of his Antiquarian researches,
And knowledge of the principles of Ecclesiastical and Civil
Architecture,
By the judicious application of this talent,
Joined to a firm but mild execution of his official authority,
He greatly contributed to the decent and substantial restoration
Of many venerable fabrics within his Archdeaconry.
His "Account of the Ancient and Present State of Shrewsbury,"
Originally published in a single volume,
Was afterwards embodied in a complete History written by him,
In conjunction with the Rev. John Brickdale Blakeway.
He died Dec. 23d, 1827, aged 67 years.
Harriet, his wife, daughter of Edward Jeffreys, Esq.
Died April 3d, 1825, aged 59 years.

In the south aisle, a plain tablet surmounted by a lion commemorates the public spirit and unremitting exertions of Mr. ROBERT LAWRENCE, " in opening the great road through Wales between the united kingdoms, and for establishing the first mail coach to this town." He died Sept. 3d, 1806, aged 57 years.

The living is a perpetual curacy in the presentation of the Right Hon. the Earl of Tankerville, and the parish comprehends the Wyle Cop and the suburb of Coleham, but isolated districts of it are intermixed with several of the other parishes at different ends of the town.

A Sunday evening lecture was commenced at this church, April 20th, 1828, for the " free accommodation of the town at large," the parishioners having consented to lend their pews for the occasion. Several of the clergy connected with the town preach alternately at this additional service.

THE PARISH OF
ST. MICHAEL WITHIN THE CASTLE.

It has been already stated (page 24) that the royal free chapel of St. Juliana became at an early period appurtenant to the church of St. Michael, the situation of which it has been shown was within the castle.

It is uncertain whether a church existed here anterior to the Norman conquest; however, in the survey called Domesday-book, compiled in 1085, the churches of Shrewsbury are mentioned in the following order, and their possessions enumerated: viz. St. Mary, St. Michael, St. Chad, St. Alkmund, and St. Julian. And of St. Michael these particulars are given:

" The Church of Saint Michael holds, of the Earl Roger, *Posseton:* Chetel held it [in the time of the Confessor]: there is one virgate of land : the land is half a carucate : one man renders therefore a bundle of box on the day of Palms. The same church holds *Suletene:* Brictric, a free man held it from the Confessor, when there was one hide paying tax at the time of the Conquest: the land was one caracute: there was also half a carucate: it was then worth five shillings; now (the completion of Domesday) four pence less.*

It may be useful, therefore, in this place to relate some further information respecting the parish of St. Michael, which has lately excited the public attention, by the parish of St. Mary enforcing a demand for the payment of poor-rates upon the tenant of the Castle, J. C. Pelham, Esq. and which that gentleman resisted on the ground that the Castle formed no part of the parish of St. Mary. The issue came on for trial at the Summer Assizes, 1836, before Mr. Justice Patteson and a special jury, when a verdict was obtained in favour of the plaintiff, Mr. Pelham.

1222.—This Chapel was of the donation of the Lord the King, and given to William de Haverhul.

The Chapel of the Forde was also of the gift of the King, and belonged to this church of the Castle, and rendered three shillings, and was worth one mark, which William de Haverhul then held.

1235.—The Chapel of St. Michael was held by William de Battal, and was worth yearly fourteen marks.

1271.—The Rector of St. Michael proceeded to recover in law for services due to him in right of his church. The entry commences thus:

" Robert Corbet, of Morton, offered himself on the fourth day (fourth day probably of the assizes at Shrewsbury) against Richard de Sarre, Parson of the Church of St. Michael, of a plea that the same Robert should do to the aforesaid Richard the accustomed and right services which

G 2

* These possessions were about 150 acres.

he ought to do to him for his frank tenement which he holds of him in *Soleton* and Lack.

1293.—The Chapel of St. Michael was worth yearly twelve marks, and Master Adam de Malane held it of the gift of the King.

1309.—King Edward the Second granted to his beloved clerk, Boniface de Ledes, this Free Chapel, vacant by the resignation of Roger de Ledes.

1318.—A similar Grant to Roger de Lysewy, of this Free Chapel of St. Michael, being then vacant, &c. To this grant is appended an order from the King to " Master Thomas de Cherlton," then Constable of the Castle, to induct this Roger into corporal possession thereof.

1330.—A similar Grant of this Chapel, being vacant, to Walter de London.

1330.—A subsequent Grant, in this year, of the said Chapel to Adam de Overton.

1342.—It appears that Adam D'Overton was Warden of this Free Chapel of St. Michael.

1343.—A Grant to John de Wynwyk of this Free Chapel, and an order to John de Wyndsore, then the Constable, to induct him ; also a Grant to the same John de Wynwyk of the King's Free Chapel of St. Julian, Salop.

1344.—A Grant to John Fitz John Le Strange, of Blaunkmonstr, of this Free Chapel.

1347.—It appears that a suit was pending between John Fitz John Le Strange, of Whitechurch, Parson of this Free Chapel, and certain persons in the pleas mentioned.

1395.—An Inquisition taken at Salop, on Wednesday next after the Exaltation of the Holy Cross, before John de Eyton, Sheriff of Salop, by virtue of a certain Writ to the said Sheriff directed, and to this Inquisition annexed, by oath of William Banaster of Bromdon, and others, who say upon their oath that William Tyrington, late Parson of this Chapel, had committed waste, dilapidation, and destruction in this Chapel, to wit, in throwing down, dilapidating, and destroying this Chapel, to the value of one hundred pounds, through the defect of the roofing, repairing, and supporting of this Chapel, that is, in lead, stone, timber, and glass windows, and also in the carrying away one chalice and divers entire vestments, with all the ornaments ordained for the said chalice and vestments pertaining to the said Chapel, and by destroying divers images lately being in the same Chapel, by reason of his improvident custody of the said Chapel, and of his neglect of the repairing of this Chapel, to the value aforesaid, beginning the defects aforesaid in the Feast of Easter, in the 48th year of King Edward the Third, till the death of this William Tyrington, so that this Chapel was utterly destroyed and wholly thrown down and laid in ruins by this William de Tyrington, late Parson of this Chapel, and so that two hundred marks were not sufficient to amend and repair it, with the ornaments lately being therein.

1410.—A Grant by King Henry the Fourth, reciting, that whereas he had granted to "Roger Yve, of Leeton, Rector of our Chapel of St. John the Baptist at Adbrighton Husee," "certain lands in fields called the Batteleyfield, in which field the battle between us and Henry Percy, deceased, and certain of our rebels, lately took place," in order to build "a certain Chapel of St. Mary Magdalene," of which he was appointed Warden, with power to choose five Chaplains to celebrate Divine Service in the said Chapel every day. The Grant then proceeds to endow the said Chapel of St. Mary Magdalene at Battlefield with various possessions, and among others with the Advowson of "the King's Free Chapel of St. Michael within the Castle of Salop, to which the Chapel of St. Julian of Salop is appurtenant or appendant."

1417.—John Repynton, then Warden of the said Chapel of Saint Michael, surrendered the same to the King.

1558.—John Halliwell took of Richard Burper, among other property, all manner of tithes, oblations, obventions, fruits, profits, and emoluments, of the Rectory, Church, and Chapel, of Saint Julian, and of " the Chapel of Saint Michael."

1583.—Was a Fine, passing the same property.

Queen Elizabeth having granted a lease of the Castle and its appurtenances to Humphrey Onslow, Esq. at the yearly rent of 13s. 4d. that gentleman's lease expired in 1596, when the Castle and its appurtenances came into the possession of the Corporation.

In the records of the Corporation is the following entry :

1605.—" Agreed that persons shall view the stones in the Castle belonging to St. Michael's Chapel, and take account thereof, and enquire what stones are taken away."

There can be little doubt, however, but the Parish of St. Michael's had originally some connexion with St. Mary's parish ; for in the reign of Henry II. it seems that Walter de Dunstanville, Rector of St. Michael's, sold a tract of land called Wogheresforlong and a moiety of Derefold to a person named Gilbert, reserving to himself a rent of three shlllings and sixpence ; and that John the son of Gilbert soon afterwards conveyed it to one Nicholas le Poncer, who subsequently granted it to Haghmond Abbey, free from all secular service, saving a rent of four shillings to be annually paid (in lieu of the tithes of Derefold) to the parson of the parish of the church of St. Michael within the Castle.

This commutation is assented to and witnessed by the Dean and Chapter of St. Mary's, " for us and our successors for ever;" an attestation which would appear as quite unnecessary, if this district had not once been connected with their jurisdiction.

The etymology of Derfald, or Deerfold, is an enclosure or park (which will be noticed hereafter) for keeping deer, an appendage not unusual to our early fortresses. This circumstance (and at a period when little respect was shown to boundaries civil or ecclesiastical) might have induced Roger de Montgomery, as feudal lord, to assign it as the parochial limits of his church, although at the cost of the parish of St. Mary.

THE ABBEY CHURCH.

THE ABBEY CHURCH is situated in the suburb to which it has given the name of Abbey Foregate. It is built of a deep red stone. A noble simplicity combined with a massive solidity characterizes the whole structure, to which time has given a most venerable appearance; and, though marks of mutilation are too evident throughout, it displays many curious features of ancient Norman architecture combined with the earlier pointed style.

It originally formed part of the richly endowed monastery founded in 1083 by Roger de Montgomery, Earl of Shrewsbury, and when entire was a stately cruciform building, equal in size to some of our cathedrals, having a central and western tower, transepts, &c. The whole eastern portion, two-thirds of the structure, was barbarously destroyed at the dissolution of monasteries in the time of Henry the Eighth. The neglect of after-times has contributed much to disfigure its external elevation, the eastern portion of the upper clerestory having from decay fallen down some time about the close of the 17th century.

The present church consists of the nave, side aisles, and western tower of the Abbey church, and owes its escape to the circumstance of the western end having always been used as the church of the parish of HOLY CROSS, the name it still retains.

The west front is composed of the tower, flanked by the ends of the Norman side aisles, and has a bold appearance. The tower is broad and massive; the basement early Norman, surmounted by a well-proportioned superstructure of the 14th century. The portal is a deeply recessed round-headed arch, having a pointed doorway inserted within it; to preserve uniformity, the exterior rib of the outward round arch springs on each side from a Norman shaft with an indented capital, and the combination displays much skill and ingenuity.

Above this is one of the most magnificent windows in the kingdom, 46 feet high by 23 feet wide; the intrado of the arch is enriched by a series of small trefoil panels; the label rises high above it in the ogee form, richly crocketed and terminated in a finial. The window is in the decorated style, and divided horizontally by transoms, and perpendicularly by six mullions, into seven compartments for the glass, the lower division having blank panels which have never been pierced for glazing. The arched head is gracefully pointed and filled with a profusion of the most rich and delicate tracery.

On each side of the window are the remains of a canopied niche, which once contained statues, probably of Saint Peter and St. Paul, the tutelar saints of the Abbey.

The north and south-west angles of the tower are flanked by shelving buttresses, having their sets-off worked into pedimented weatherings. The bell chamber has two windows on each side, between those of the western front is an elegant canopied niche containing the statue of an armed knight, bearing in one hand a mutilated sword, the other appears to have once projected from the body, but is now broken. The figure has a conical basinet, encircled by a crown, fastened to a camail of mail, which covers the neck, shoulders, and breast to the hips, and is finished by an emblazoned jupon. The thighs and legs are encased in plate armour. This statue is supposed to represent Edward the Third, in whose reign the tower was probably built.

On the north side of the church is a lofty and handsome porch, the entrance to which is under a pointed arch resting on round columns, and peculiarly recessed within a square aperture charged with shields; above is a chamber (formerly in two stories) lighted by small mullioned windows whose arches are nearly flat. On each side are niches, in one of which is the remains of a figure. The ceiling of the porch is cylindrical, without ornament, and the interior doorway a plain semi-circular arch with round mouldings.

The exterior of the side aisles displays a series of modern gables, each of which contains a mullioned window. The eastern end of the church is finished by a wall run up between the remains of the two western piers that supported a central tower, in which a pointed window is inserted. This, however, will soon be removed, and three elegant Norman lights substituted by private munificence.

On the south side the gables are at present miserably repaired with brickwork, but it is to be hoped that ere long the public spirit and good taste of the town will be exercised in such a manner as to assist the parishioners in the proper restoration of this side of the church, which presents so striking a feature from the new line of the London road.

The south aisle is entered by a plain Norman arch, resting on slender shafts, and which once communicated with the western wing of the cloister; the approach from the opposite eastern wing was by a pointed doorway; adjoining this is the ruined wall of the transept, in which are two round arches, supposed to have formed portions of a side aisle, or small chantry chapel west of the transept.

THE INTERIOR

presents a majestic appearance of solemnity, calculated t raise devout and profound veneration towards that AI MIGHTY BEING to whose service and honour the edifice i. dedicated, as well as to enchain the attention to the scriptural motto inscribed upon the north portal—" REVERENCI MY SANCTUARY."

The nave is separated from the side aisles by five arches : two, which on each side join the tower, are in the pure style of the 14th century, and delicately lined with deep mouldings resting on clustered columns, and exhibit very distinctly the taste which prevailed in engrafting the more elegant pointed upon the massy Anglo-Norman style; the former, it will be clearly seen, have been formed out of the original semi-circular arches, similar to the three eastward, which rest on short thick round pillars ($16\frac{1}{2}$ feet in circumference) of the plainest Norman character. Above these is a story of smaller arches in the same style, now filled up, but which evidently shew that it was the intention of the monastery to assimilate them to the style adopted in the side windows of the tower and western portion of the nave : the alteration, however, was not completed.

The pointed arch opposite the north porch is partly filled by a skreen, the remnant of a small chantry chapel which formerly occupied this portion of the church. This skreen is adorned with a series of foliated niches once enriched with sculpture.

The ceiling of the church is painted in imitation of an oak ribbed roof, ornamented with flowers, the intersections of the ribs being finished with bosses, and the interstices with quatrefoils. A lofty beautiful pointed arch, 52 feet high, springing from richly moulded imposts divides the tower from the nave, by which the whole front of the great western window is displayed. This window is filled with a series of armorial bearings in stained glass, restored in 1814 at the expence and under the direction of the Rev. W. G. Rowland, M. A. from a drawing in the Heralds' College.

First row : 1. Beauchamp ; 2. Thomas of Woodstock, Duke of Gloucester ; 3. King Richard the Second ; 4. John of Gaunt, Duke of Lancaster ; 5. Edmund of Langley, Duke of York ; 6. Stafford.

Second row : 7. Audley ; 8. Clare ; 9. B. a lion rampant O. (the arms of the monastery); 10. Barry of twelve, A. and S.

Third row: 11. Mortimer Earl of March; 12. Fitz-alan and Warren.

Fourth row: 13. Montague; 14. Boteler of Wem; 15. Ufford Earl of Suffolk; 16. B. on a bend A. three escallops S.

Fifth row: 17. Warren Earl of Surrey; 18, 19, 20. B. a lion rampant within a bordure O. (probably intended for the three Norman Earls of Shrewsbury); 21. Blunde-ville Earl of Chester; 22. Sir Philip de Burnell.

Sixth row: 23. England and France quarterly; 24. John of Hainault; 25. Strange of Blackmere; 26. Strange of Knockin; 27. Lisle; 28. Mortimer Earl of March; 29. Arundel and Warren; 30. France semée and England; 31. Arundel and Maltravers; 32. Corbet; 33. Albini; 34. Latimer; 35. Roger de Montgomery; 36. Sir Simon de Burley impaling Stafford; which last bearings will probably fix the date when the original window was put up, viz. about the 12th of King Richard the Second.

The whole extent of the tower is occupied by a spacious gallery, in which is an excellent organ made by Gray, of London, and erected in 1806 at a cost of 365 guineas. The front of the gallery is a gothic skreen of three arches, divided by buttresses, and displays the armorial bearings of the principal benefactors to the organ.

The eastern window contains six resplendent figures in stained glass, executed by Mr. David Evans, of Shrewsbury, viz. St. James, King David, St. John, King Solomon (as in the act of consecrating the Temple), St. Peter, and St. Paul, with their respective emblems. The figures were placed in rich tracery work in 1836, but the window was originally set up in 1820, with the following inscription:—AEDI . SANCTAE . CRUCIS . Post . Annos . Viginti . Septem . In . SACRIS . EJUS . Administrandis . Impensos .

Dono . Dedit . Gvlielmvs . Gorsvch . Rowland . anno . salvtis . MDCCCXX.

Below this window is a series of highly-enriched Norman arches, forming the altar skreen, erected from a design by Mr. Carline, and at the expense of the Rev. Richard Scott, B. D. which has given a most imposing feature to this part of the church.

The north-east window was the gift of the late Lord Berwick, and previously to the year 1820 stood over the altar. In the centre compartment is a large figure of St. Peter, and the remainder of the window is occupied by the arms of the See of Lichfield, those of the munificent donor, and thirteen escutcheons of the incumbents from the Reformation to 1804. A rich border lines the mullions, and at the bottom is inscribed—MVNIFICENTIA . VIRI . PRAE-NOBILIS . THOMAE . NOEL . BARONIS . BERWICK . DE . ATTINGHAM . HVJVS . ECCLESIAE . PATRONI . ANNO . SALV-TIS . MDCCCVI.

Small windows divided by a single mullion are placed in the eastern arches of the side aisles (which formerly opened with the transepts); that on the north side has the arms of Mortimer, Fitzalan, Talbot, and Berkeley, in stained glass. The corresponding window of the south aisle has three ancient shields (originally in the great chamber of the abbey) bearing the arms of France and England, Roger de Montgomery, and the symbols of the Patron Saints, the key and sword, in saltire.

In the south aisle is a beautiful mosaic window of stained glass, by Mr. D. Evans, containing twelve shields of the armorial bearings of families connected with the late Rev. John Rocke. Underneath is inscribed—MAJORVM SVORVM INSIGNIA DEPINGI CURAVIT JOHANNES ROCKE, MDCCCXX.

The western portion of the south aisle is walled from the church for a vestry, near which, on a pavement of emblazoned tiles, stands the Font: the pedestal is carved with zigzag mouldings, and supports a round basin, ornamented with chevron work and small arched panels. This originally belonged to the church at High Ercall.

Another font, found some years since in the adjoining garden, is at the eastern end of the north aisle. Its basin represents an open flower, over which is festooned drapery supported from the mouths of grotesque heads; the pillar on which it is fixed formed the upper part of the ancient cross which formerly stood opposite the south door of St. Giles's church. On the sides are sculptured the Crucifixion, the Visitation, the Virgin and Child, and a person in the act of devotion.

Length of the church from east to west 123 feet, breadth (including aisles) 63 feet; the tower is 104 feet in height, and contains a fine mellow peal of eight bells.

MONUMENTS—SOUTH AISLE.

The oldest monument in the church is the mutilated cumbent figure of a warrior clad in mail of the date of King John's reign, and conjectured by the heralds at the visitation in 1623 to be the effigy of the Founder of the abbey, who died July 27th, 1094. It has been placed on a basement of early pointed arches, by the Rev. W. G. Rowland, M.A. to whose taste this church is mainly indebted for its interior beauty and interest.

On the fall of St. Chad's and the demolition of St. Alkmund's church, several ancient monuments found an habitation within the aisles of this church. To enumerate all the inscriptions on these and other memorials would far exceed the prescribed limits of these pages: a brief survey must therefore suffice.

Commencing at the eastern end of the south aisle, we find—a bust, under a Roman arch, in alderman's robes, representing John Lloyd, alderman of this town, who died in 1647, aged 53.

Near this is a handsome altar-tomb bearing two cumbent figures, an alderman in his civic robes, with picked beard and bareheaded, and a lady in a scarlet gown, finished after the stiff habit of the times, denoting William Jones and Eleanor his wife; the former died in 1612, and the latter in 1623. These were brought from St. Alkmund's.

An alabaster tomb from Wellington old church, described by Dugdale as " a faire raised monument, whereon is cut the portraiture of a man in armour, and by him his wife, with this inscription"—

Hic jacet in Tumba corpus Will'mi Chorlton armigeri et Anne Uxor' ejus; que quidem Anna obiit vii die mensis Junii, Anno D'ni Mill'imo ccccxxiiii. et dictus Will'ms obiit p'mo die mensis Julii anno d'ni mill'imo ccccxliiii. quorum animab' p'picietur Deus.

On the sides of the tomb are a series of canopied niches, with figures of angels and friars bearing shields, on which are emblazoned armorial bearings of the families of *Charlton*, *Zouch*, and *Horde*; one of the friars is remarkable, having a fox's head peeping out from under his long gown.

In this part are handsome mural tablets with Latin inscriptions to the memory of individuals of the families of ROCKE, PRINCE, BALDWIN, &c. &c.

Near the south entrance is the cumbent figure of a cross-legged knight in linked armour, with surcoat, sword in scabbard, gauntlets on his hands, spurs on his heels, and his feet resting on a lion. It is considered to be the effigy of *Sir Walter de Dunstanville*, Lord of Ideshale, and a benefactor to Wombridge Priory, from whence the figure was brought. He died 25th Henry III.

NORTH AISLE.

Resting on a basement is a curious ancient ridge-backed gravestone, on which is cut a foliated cross; under this is a small figure clad as a priest, close to whose head is attached the outline of a bell. On the right side is a chalice, a book, and a candle; round the edge of the stone is T : M : O : R : E : U : A, which is conjectured to mean Thomas More, Vicarius Abbatiæ. It was removed from St. Giles's.

Among other ancient cumbent figures in this aisle, one is supposed to represent a Judge who died in Shrewsbury, being robed to the feet, and having a coif drawn close over his head, and tied under the chin. It is of the date of Edward I.

Another monumental statue clad in plate armour displays a long loose robe as the surcoat, which is curiously disposed on one side to shew the warlike character of the deceased, whose armour, belt, and dagger would have been otherwise concealed. The head is wrapped in a close cowl. From the peculiarity of the robe being thrown back, this effigy is probably unique. Froissart asserts that a similar dress was worn in battle, and that this kind of long loose drapery proved fatal to Sir John Chandos, for he " wore over his armour a large robe which fell to ye ground;" and as it appears, when he marched " entangled his legs so that he made a stumble, and was killed by the enemy." The costume of the present figure (which originally stood on an altar-tomb in St. Alkmund's church) may be attributed to the close of the 14th century; but whom it represents is now unknown.

On the side walls are several neat tablets. An elegant canopied niche with pinnacles commemorates Edward Jenkins, Esq. of Charlton Hill, co. Salop, who ably distinguished himself in the first American war, being then a lieutenant in the 60th regiment, and died May 1, 1820, in his 81st year.

At the eastern end is a large altar-tomb, on which are recumbent figures of Richard Onslow, Esq. (Speaker of the House of Commons in the reign of Elizabeth), and his lady Catherine; the former is dressed in his robes of office, and the latter in the dress of the times. On the sides and ends of the monument are small figures of his sons and daughters. He died in 1571, and was buried at St. Chad's.

Above this is a mural monument representing a gentleman and lady kneeling opposite to each other under a rich Grecian entablature; the former is clad in a ruff and long gown, and the latter has a long veil thrown back. They represent Thomas Edwards, Esq. who died 1634, and Ann his wife, daughter of Humfrey Baskerville, alderman of London. Over the entablature is a lady in a richly-laced habit, and a little girl kneeling, intended for Mary, wife of Thomas Edwards, Esq. and daughter of Thomas Bonham Norton, Esq. who died in childbirth, 1641.

In the vestry is an old painting of the Crucifixion, which was a century ago " turned out of the church," and occasioned at the time some strife between the parson and his flock.

The living is a vicarage, with St. Giles's annexed, in the gift of the Right Hon. Lord Berwick, who received it from the Crown in exchange for three small livings in Suffolk.

The ruins of the monastic buildings, which are now scattered over an extent of about nine acres, are not considerable, and will be described in a notice of the suburb of Abbey-foregate.

SAINT GILES'S CHURCH.

Sacred edifices, under the invocation of this Saint, were generally founded "without the city;" that in this town occupies a situation at the eastern extremity of the suburb of Abbey-foregate.

The structure is unquestionably as old as the early part of the twelfth century; and while presenting an interesting picture of the work of former times, has a tendency to lead the mind, under fit impressions, to the hope of a less perishable, " greater, and more perfect tabernacle."

It consists of a nave, chancel, and north aisle, with a small turret at the western end, in which a bell has lately been introduced. The principal entrance is at the south, under a Norman arch. The north aisle is separated from the nave by three pointed arches sustained on plain round columns, formed (it appears) in the thickness of the wall, and peculiarly flanked on the north side by square piers, having an upper and lower narrow moulding adorned with recessed quatrefoils. These piers, it is presumed, originally served as buttresses to strengthen the outward wall of the fabric, which on receiving the addition of a north aisle (evidently at a very early period), a communication was then opened with the nave by perforating the wall into arches which are of the era when the Norman was giving way to the pointed style. It is not improbable but this aisle was made for the accommodation of persons afflicted with leprosy, to which they had access from the adjoining hospital by a pointed doorway, and where they might hear the offices of religion without endangering other worshippers with their contagious malady. At the east end is a curious round-headed window with mullions.

A fine pointed arch separates the nave from the chancel, which is terminated by a flat-arched mullioned window, containing a noble collection of stained glass, executed by Mr. David Evans, of Shrewsbury. The four lower compartments have full-length figures of THE EVANGELISTS, standing upon hexagonal pedestals, through the external circular arches of which is exhibited the groined roof of a crypt supported by slender pillars. Over each figure is a beautiful canopy of tabernacle work, and in the intersections of the tracery are the symbols of the Evangelists, each supporting a tablet, on which is respectively inscribed, in small characters—

> Mattheus Christi stirpem et genus ordine narrat
> Marcus Baptistam clamantem inducit eremo
> Virgine prognatum Lucas describit Jesum
> Prodit Joannes verbi impenetrabile lumen.

The three principal compartments in the upper division display fine representations from ancient designs of THE SALUTATION, THE WISE MENS' OFFERING, and THE PRESENTATION IN THE TEMPLE, beneath each of which is a Latin text: the first is taken from Luke i. 28; the second from Psalm lxxii. 10; the third from Luke ii. 29, 30. At the bottom of the window, GULIELMUS GORSUCH ROWLAND DONO DEDIT.

The small Norman loop-hole on the north side contains a figure of St. Giles, and is an exquisite imitation of ancient stained glass.

On the south side of the chancel is a low pointed arch, the stone-work of which projects outside the building, and was no doubt originally intended to contain the remains of a master of the hospital. After the plaister had been removed in 1826, which brought to view this archway, the ground at its base was opened, when a stone grave cased with brick-work was discovered, with part of the bones of two individuals. In 1685 it appears to have been used for the interment of the individual whose name is inscribed on the stone, and to prevent (if possible) that ejection of himself which must have befallen the remains of a former tenant, it is further added

> STVR NOT MY BONES
> WHICH ARE LAYDE IN CLAYE
> FOR I MVST RISE AT
> THE RESVRRECTION DAY.

THE INTERIOR OF THE CHURCH

Possesses much of its primitive character, being unen-
cumbered with pews, and until the last few years exhibited
a still more rude appearance of damp and neglect. Many
important improvements, however, have been effected
within and around the building, especially in placing drains
around the exterior, which have not only rendered the
interior free from damp, but contributed also to the dry-

ness of the cemetery. The alterations in the nave consist in levelling and repairing the floor, ceiling the roof, and appropriately colouring the walls and rafters ; removing the pulpit from the corner of the fine arch leading into the chancel to the south-east corner of the nave, and placing stone tracery of a bold design in the large pointed window of the south wall. The windows of the north aisle are filled with fragments of stained glass ingeniously disposed, so as to represent the outline of figures.*

In fact, whoever has visited this ancient church during its former wretched state will be astonished; it now truly looks

> " As though we own'd a God, adored his power,
> Rever'd his wisdom, loved his mercy."

And its sacred walls will, it is to be hoped, no more echo with the twittering of birds,—the sparrow find a place of security over the altar, or the swallow be permitted to " build her brooding nest" above its antique pulpit ; altho' these are striking resemblances of the tranquillity and peace which the means of grace are to a christian, and which seem to inhabit the house of the Deity.

But the sentiment which this venerable place impressed was in some measure checked by its disuse, divine service being only celebrated within its walls twice a year.

Since the foregoing account was written, the author of these Memorials has the pleasure to record that regular service was commenced in this church on Sunday, June 19, 1836, which will form a great convenience to the increasing population of the neighbourhood. Nine new oak pews have been subsequently erected within its walls, from a design by Mr. Carline, and at the expence of the Reverend

---

* A notice of the improvements in this church will be found in vol. 100, part II. of the Gent. Mag. communicated by the author of these Memorials.

Richard Scott, B. D. who has also contributed a sum that will, with the letting of the pews, further increase the stipend of a minister. Much has been very justly said against the deformity which the introduction of pews has rendered to churches; those, however, placed in this structure meet every objection, and are perfect models of what pews should be,—fixed forms having backs, but without doors ;—adapted for a devotional rather than a lounging posture. On the outside partition of each is a small carved finial, and the whole are in unison with the style of the church and ancient benches still remaining on the south side. A new altar-piece has been placed above the communion-table : the latter was presented by an inhabitant of the parish, and the former by Mr. Scott.

The dimensions of the church are—nave 45 feet by 36, chancel 20 feet by 15, total length 65 feet. The font is the upper portion of a Norman pillar with the capital hollowed, and originally belonged to the Abbey church.

It may be mentioned, that after the monks of Shrewsbury had obtained possession of the bones of St. Wenefrede in 1137, those precious relics were deposited on the altar of this church, until a shrine worthy their reception could be prepared in the Abbey.

On the floor are several ancient stones bearing crosses, no doubt denoting the interment of some of the masters of the old hospital of St. Giles.

A spacious cemetery surrounds the building, where the contemplative mind,

" Free from noise and riot rude,"

may resort, and, unmolested by the vulgar gaze of unsympathizing intruders, pour the grateful tribute of a sigh, or embalm afresh the memory of that departed spirit with whom he once took generous and undesigning counsel;

and renew in imagination, through time's dim mist, hours consecrated to friendship.

In this silent repository are gravestones 200 years old, many inhabitants of the town having selected it as their last resting place, from a feeling similar to that inscribed upon a tomb in the south-west corner of the church-yard:

Ut Nemini noceret Mortuus,
Qui Unicuique pro re nata succurrere voluit Vivus,
Hic extra Urbem sese contumulandum præcipiebat,
CHENEY HART, M. D.
Warringtoni in agro Lancastriensi natus Nov. 17-28, 1726.

A stone near the south window covers the remains of John Whitfield, surgeon, on which is recorded an epitaph, the very quintessence of chemical brevity—

I. W.
COMPOSITA SOLVANTUR.

Opposite the south door is the socket of an ancient stone cross, the upper portion of which supports a font in the Abbey church.

From hence likewise is an extensive view of the town, with the different churches displayed to much picturesque advantage, the vale below being watered by the meanderings of the Rea brook; while the more distant prospect, chequered with mountains and woody knolls, verdant pastures and rural habitations, presents a striking picture of

" Life's fair landscape, mark'd with light and shade."

SAINT MICHAEL'S CHURCH

Stands on a pleasant site in the populous suburb of Castle
Foregate.   The western side commands an interesting view
of the town.   The venerable Castle with its towers and
hoary walls, the Royal Free Grammar School, and the
lofty spires of St. Mary's and St. Alkmund's churches,
combine to form a most pleasing group; whilst the fine
church of Saint Chad, backed by distant mountains, stands

prominent in the front. On the northern side of the building is a picturesque dell, along which the majestic Severn formerly poured its crystal stream.

The church is a respectable building in the Doric style, composed of brick. It was erected by subscription, and consecrated for divine worship August 24th, 1830.

In plan, it consists of a tower, nave, side aisles, and an elliptical recess for the communion, with a vestry in the base of the tower.

The tower is of three divisions, and rises to the height of 70 feet; the basement is square, on which rests an octagonal belfry, crowned by a similar division of smaller dimensions, having a cornice charged with lions' heads, the whole being surmounted by an angular lead roof and a gilded cross.

The body of the church is in length 70 ft. 6 in. and in breadth 40 ft. 6 in. and has a stone plinth, cornice, and parapet. The windows throughout are circular-headed, having unbroken stone dressings surrounding them.

THE INTERIOR is approached by two entrances, north and south, beneath a stone cornice sustained on pilasters; and, if not splendid in decoration, it has that solemnity which becometh the House of God: it possesses, however, one great advantage, in being capable of comfortably accommodating a congregation of 800 persons, 620 of whom may possess free sittings. On the floor are thirty-six pews, the other part being entirely free. There are galleries over the north and south aisles, and at the western end, the whole of which are free sittings. These galleries are sustained on cast-iron columns, which are also continued for the support of the roof.

The ceiling has a good effect, being panelled in large square compartments, and beautifully painted in imitation of oak. The pulpit and reading desk are octagonal, and are placed on opposite sides of the church.

The eastern end is finished by three panels, inscribed with the Decalogue, &c. Three windows of splendid stained glass decorate the chancel. The subject of the centre one is the NATIVITY, from the celebrated " La Notte" of Correggio, and is a most masterly production of the art of glass-staining, especially in the management of light suitable to the time and scene of the subject. Underneath is the inscription in Roman capitals—"AND THEY CAME WITH HASTE, AND FOUND MARY, AND JOSEPH, AND THE BABE LYING IN A MANGER."

The windows on each side of the above are designed from the ANNUNCIATION, and the PRESENTATION IN THE TEMPLE, the former from a painting by Guido in the chapel of the palace on the Monte Cavallo of Rome. The angel, a beautiful figure arrayed in yellow drapery tastefully displayed, is in the act of presenting to the virgin a lily, while his attitude and countenance seem to bespeak the emphatic words of the motto inscribed beneath—"HAIL ! THOU THAT ART HIGHLY FAVOURED AMONG WOMEN ; THE LORD IS WITH THEE." The other is from the celebrated picture at Antwerp, by Rubens, and founded on the words of holy Simeon—" LORD, NOW LETTEST THOU THY SERVANT DEPART IN PEACE: ACCORDING TO THY WORD."

These windows, perfect gems of the art, were executed by Mr. David Evans, of Shrewsbury, and were the gift of the Rev. W. G. Rowland, M.A. Minister and Official of St. Mary's.

There is a small but excellent organ in the west gallery, and the tower contains a light peal of six bells, cast in 1830. The architect of the church was Mr. J. Carline ; and when it is considered that it was erected at an expence of little more than £2000, criticism is disarmed in the substantial appearance which it possesses.

The cemetery surrounding the church is particularly neat; a gravel walk extends along its sides, and the ground is laid out in divisions for graves and vaults, which are numbered according to a plan kept with the sexton.

This church is in St. Mary's parish, with the minister of which the presentation is vested.

SAINT GEORGE'S CHURCH.

SAINT GEORGE'S CHURCH is situated at the upper end

of the suburb of Frankwell, and is dedicated to the tutelar saint of England, from its proximity to the site of an ancient religious foundation called in old writings " The free chapel of St. George."

The present church was consecrated January 30th, 1832, and is cruciform in plan, having a small tower rising at the west end; it is built with fine Grinshill stone, from a design by Mr. Haycock. The architecture adopted throughout the building, with the exception of the tower, is of the lancet or early pointed style.

The west front is of three divisions guarded by projecting buttresses, the centre portion forming the principal entrance, a pointed arch bounded by a sweeping label; above this is a lancet light, succeeded by a panel intended for a clock dial. From this part the tower shows itself above the roof to the height of about 20 feet, and has mullioned windows in the style of the 16th century, surmounted by an embattled parapet and four crocketed pinnacles crowned with finials. The flanks of the west end are quite plain, having in their centre narrow blank loopholes.

The nave has on each side four lancet windows, bounded by labels; and the northern and southern extremities of the transepts, with the chancel or eastern end, have triple lancet windows with recessed mouldings, resting on grotesque carved heads. The transepts and chancel terminate with gables, having on their apex a crocketed pinnacle.

The extreme length of the church is about 84 feet, and 30 feet in width, the transepts from north to south are 66 feet, and the tower to the summit of the pinnacles 60 feet.

THE INTERIOR

possesses a very pleasing appearance.   The basement of

I 3

the tower forms the vestibule, which is flanked on one side by the vestry, and on the other by the stairs leading to the gallery. The aisles of the nave and transepts are occupied by free benches, with a passage on either hand, the pews being placed along the side walls of the entire building.

The font is of free-stone, and placed on a pedestal in the area between the transepts; the basin is octangular, having on its side compartments a small quatrefoil sunk within a square panel.

On each side of the communion table are two carved gothic chairs; and nearly the whole extent of the eastern wall of the chancel is covered with a handsome altar skreen.

The three lancet windows are filled with splendid stained glass.

The subject occupying the centre window is a full-length figure of ISAIAH, in an attitude strikingly prophetic, and clothed in a brilliant vest of purple, over which is thrown a green robe lined with ermine, denoting his royal descent.

The corresponding windows on each side have spirited figures of ST. MATTHEW and ST. MARK. The former exhibits deep and serious meditation, with a most benign countenance; in his right hand is a halbert, and in his left a Greek manuscript. ST. MARK is a most venerable figure, whose head appears covered with the frost of hoary years, and he is pointing to an open gospel which he holds in his left hand.

The figures stand on rich bases, which display an highly ornamented quatrefoil, and are surmounted by canopies of the most elegant crocketed tabernacle work, which have a truly pleasing effect.

At the base of the window is a series of pointed arches in ruby glass, beneath which is the following inscription:

HANC . FENESTRAM . PICTURATAM . AEDIS . SANCTI . GEOR-

GII . DECORANDAE . ERGO . DONAVIT . RICARDUS . SCOTT .
SACRAE . THEOLOGIAE . BACCALAUREUS . ANNO . SALUTIS .
MDCCCXXXIII.

The triple windows of the north and south transepts
are also embellished by the same benefactor with elegant
mosaic patterns of elaborate workmanship, vying in richness and mellowness of colouring with the finest specimens
of ancient stained glass.

The taste displayed in the execution of these windows
is highly creditable to the talents of our townsman, Mr.
David Evans, and will, we trust, long remain as a noble
example of private generosity.

Attached to the west end is a deep gallery of free seats,
which contains a small organ, presented by the Rev. Richard
Scott, B.D. in 1834.

The church was erected by a public subscription and
a grant from the commissioners for building churches.
The total cost, exclusive of the site, was nearly £4000, of
which sum, however, £400 has been vested in the name of
trustees as a fund for future repairs.

There are 57 pews which will accommodate 290 persons, and 460 free and unappropriated sittings.

The right of presentation is in the vicar of St. Chad's.

THE OLD HOSPITAL OF ST. GEORGE stood on a site eastward between the present church and the Welsh bridge, which
latter, as early as the reign of Henry II. was called " Saint
George's Bridge." About the year 1150, the Bishop of Coventry, considering the great poverty of the brethren of the
Hospital of St. George, Salop, released to all who should
contribute to their necessities " thirteen days of penance en-
joined them, and a share of all the prayers and alms within
his Bishoprick." In 1448 the church appears to have been in
the gift of the Crown, and is supposed to have been taken down
early in the reign of Elizabeth.

TRINITY CHURCH.

The necessity of additional church accommodation for a population of 2200 persons who inhabit the SUBURB OF COLEHAM having been generally acknowledged, inasmuch as most of them were destitute of sittings in the parish church, where many of the pews are freehold, and others let at such rents as are beyond the means not only of the labouring poor (who form the greater part of the township) but of the class immediately above them, a meeting of the parishioners and others interested in the spiritual welfare of this isolated district of the town, was therefore held in the vestry of St. Julian's church, Dec. 7th, 1835, when it was resolved to be highly necessary to erect a chapel of ease in Coleham, with free sittings for at least two-thirds of the number it may contain.

A committee was formed for the purpose of carrying the proposed design into execution, and of soliciting pecuniary assistance in all proper quarters. No sooner was this announced than Salopian generosity was immediately excited, and the town and neighbourhood by their contributions, in co-operation with those of the parishioners, soon raised one thousand pounds, which has been subsequently increased by a grant of £600 from the Lichfield Diocesan Society for building churches, and a further grant of £150 from the Incorporated Church Building Society.

The parishioners of St. Julian's, desirous also of remedying the inconvenient and crowded state resulting from repeated interments in the cemetery adjoining their church during a period of one thousand years, purchased an eligible piece of land in MEOLE ROAD, for the two-fold purpose of erecting the new church and affording additional burial ground. The foundations of the church were commenced in July, 1836, and (under active management) the structure is now in rapid progress towards completion, and will be dedicated to the Holy Trinity.

The front elevation is sufficiently detailed in the foregoing vignette; the body has five windows on each side, corresponding with those in the front. The chancel is an elliptical recess, separated from the nave internally by a circular arch.

The interior is 72 feet by 46, and intended to afford 812 sittings, 500 of which will be free, having a gallery over the principal entrance.

Without further detail of the building, it may be

observed that it possesses one paramount advantage, viz. *usefulness ;* and it is to be hoped, that as the inhabitants of the suburbs of our town become possessed of greater facilities for hearing the Word of God, they may value the blessing, and support it practically by their influence and example.

The estimated cost is about £1835 ; builder, Mr. Stant. The appointment of minister is vested with the incumbent of the parish church.

––––––––

RELIGIOUS HOUSES or Chapels, in former times, stood at five different approaches into Shrewsbury : of these St. Giles's only remains.

The chapel of St. Mary Magdalene appears from the following extract to have occupied a site near Trinity church. Edward III. 5 June, 1356, granted to his beloved in Christ *Roger*, Hermit of the Chapel of St. Mary Magdalene, situated without Salop, a certain plat of waste called Spelcrosse, contiguous to the said chapel, and containing an acre of land : to hold the same to him and his successors, hermits there, for their habitation, and to find a chaplain to pray in the chapel for the king's soul, &c. A deed also of 1634 mentions " The Hermitage lane leading into Meole-field." A tea-garden near the site of " Belle Vue" was, in the recollection of many inhabitants, called " the Hermitage."

––––––––

DISSENTING MEETING HOUSES.

The first regular Presbyterian congregation formed in Shrewsbury was by the Reverends John Bryan, M. A. and the learned Francis Tallents, who were ejected by the Act of Uniformity in 1662 from the livings of St. Chad's and St. Mary's. After experiencing the various alternations of suffering and indulgence during the unsettled reign of Charles the First, and assembling for some time in private houses, they at length built a meeting house in the High-street, in 1691. But while they separated themselves from the established church on account of her discipline, they did not renounce the leading doctrines of the gospel as preserved in that church, which is evident from the inscription set up in their new building :—

"This place was not built for a faction, or a party, but to promote repentance and faith, in communion with all those who love our Lord Jesus Christ in sincerity.

"Our help is in the name of the Lord, who made heaven and earth."

The year 1715 was particularly unfortunate for the Protestant Dissenters in this and the adjoining counties: several of their places of worship were destroyed by riotous mobs raised against the king and his government. During the violence of these insurrections, the High-street meeting house was demolished, in the night of July 6th, 1715, and the pulpit publicly burnt. Government, however, speedily caused it to be rebuilt; after which the royal arms were placed within the building.

The good and pious Job Orton preached here for several years. On his resignation in 1766, a difference of sentiment arose among the members of the congregation in the choice of a minister. The building is now used for worship by the Unitarians. It is 70 feet by 30, and fitted up in the heavy style of the last century.

THE INDEPENDENTS.

The place occupied by this denomination had its origin in consequence of the schism in the High-street congregation, and is situated in a retired area on Swan-hill. It is a substantial square edifice, with a neatly finished interior. On a stone tablet in the front is the following inscription :

> " This building was erected in the year 1767, for the Public Worship of God, and in defence of the Rights of Majorities in Protestant Dissenting Congregations to choose their own Ministers."

On the north-east side is a spacious vestry, containing portraits of the Rev. Mr. Tallents and other ejected clergymen. The space adjoining three sides of the building is used as a cemetery.

BAPTISTS.

A society of this persuasion is stated to have existed in this town in the time of the Commonwealth. The meeting house, in Claremont-street, was opened in 1780, and enlarged in 1810. It contains a monument in memory of Mr. Palmer, who was pastor of the congregation 27 years, and died in 1823.

THE SECOND BAPTISTS

Seceded from the above society in 1827, and built a place for worship in Castle Foregate, which was opened April 9, 1830. They retain, however, the doctrines of Particular or Calvinistic Baptists, as professed by the former society.

THE WESLEYAN METHODISTS

Assemble on St. John's hill, in a building erected in 1804, and which was enlarged and decorated in 1825. Galleries surround the interior, in which is a small organ. The pulpit stands in the middle aisle.

A small building erected at Spring Gardens, Castle Foregate (by the proprietor of the land) was opened Feb. 26, 1826, in connexion with this society. The service is free, and the place is used at certain hours on the Sunday as a school.

THE METHODIST NEW CONNEXION

appear to claim a mutual relationship to the founder of Methodism with the Wesleyans, and retain the doctrines, ordinances, and general discipline common to that body, from which they differ only in the form of church government and professed dissent from the Church of England. This society formed a congregation here in 1833, and in Jan. 1834, an edifice for their service was commenced near the Old Tower, Murivance, which was opened June 13 in the same year.

The exterior is handsome, having two entrances with a Doric portico to each, and is divided into three parts, viz. a centre and two wings, formed with Corinthian pilasters, frieze, and cornice; the centre terminates with a pediment, and the wings with a broken blocking and Grecian tiles. The interior is without galleries, and arranged on rather a novel plan; the middle is occupied by two rows of pews, with a row on each of the sides which ascend gradually from the floor, and thereby afford great economy of space.

Two ends of the building being flanked by dwellings, light is admitted from the side portions, but a good effect, notwithstanding, is produced from the blank walls, which display arches and plain pilasters supporting a frieze aud cornice.

The ground at the back declining considerably from

K

the street, spacious school-rooms, a vestry, and a house for the door-keeper, are formed underneath the building, which is calculated to contain 700 persons, and cost £1500.

THE WELSH CALVINISTIC METHODISTS

meet in a neat structure in Hill's Lane, erected by a sub-scription on a portion of the site of a former edifice, and was opened for worship Dec. 25, 1826.   The service is in the Ancient British language.

THE PRIMITIVE METHODISTS

introduced themselves into this town in 1822, by preaching in the streets and suburbs.   The place originally built in Castle-court, Castle-street, for the Sandemanian Baptists (a society in this town nearly extinct), was purchased for them, and they commenced service there June 4th, 1826.

THE QUAKERS

have a convenient meeting-house, fitted up with much simplicity, and neatness, on St. John's Hill, to which a small burial ground is attached.

THE ROMAN CATHOLIC CHAPEL

Is situated near the southern portion of the town walls. The exterior exhibits a stuccoed pedimented front, sur-mounted by a plain cross.   The interior was enlarged in 1826, and is elegant in decoration, and calculated to contain nearly 250 persons.

ROYAL FREE GRAMMAR SCHOOL.

" Learning is an addition beyond
  Nobility of birth : honour of blood,
  Without the ornament of knowledge, is
  But a glorious ignorance."

SHIRLEY.

This noble public institution for the education of youth
was founded by KING EDWARD THE SIXTH, in 1561, on the
supplication of Henry Edwards and Richard Whitaker, and
endowed with the greater portion of the revenues of the two
dissolved colleges of Saint Mary and Saint Chad.—
QUEEN ELIZABETH greatly augmented her brother's donation in 1571, by adding the whole rectory of Chirbury, in

K 3

this county, with additional tithes and estates in St. Mary's parish, which now produce a considerable revenue.

In 1798, the School having sunk into a state of comparative insignificance, a bill was passed for the better government and regulation of the Grammar School of King Edward the Sixth in this town, by which the management of the revenues, and the removal or discharge of the masters, is vested in the Bishop of Lichfield and Coventry (as visitor) and thirteen trustees or governors.   The appointment of head and second masters rests with the Fellows of St. John's College, Cambridge.   The school is open for the gratuitous instruction of the sons of freemen, and has maintained a character of high repute from its earliest formation.   We learn that under the care of its first master, Thomas Ashton, there were 290 scholars, among whom were many of the sons of the gentry of the county and from North Wales, as well as from the first families in the kingdom.   Camden. when he wrote, says, " it was the best filled in all England, being indebted for their flourishinge state to provision made by the excellent and worthie Thomas Ashton," who was instrumental in procuring the grant of augmentation from Elizabeth, and contributed greatly to the school himself, and from whose exertions and judicious regulations it preserved its usefulness for many generations.

Many persons of eminence in by-gone days received their education in Shrewsbury School.   In the reign of Queen Elizabeth it sent forth one of the most brilliant ornaments of her court, the gallant and accomplished SYDNEY,—the " miracle of the age;"—and in the present day, under the able management and profound learning of the late head-master, Dr. Butler, it has maintained a preeminent rank among THE PUBLIC SEMINARIES OF SOUND LEARNING AND RELIGIOUS EDUCATION in this country, having produced numerous individuals who have been distinguished for their eminent classical attainments; whilst it is an acknowledged fact that scarcely any gentleman can be pointed out who has sent so many pupils to the Universities, the greater part of whom have risen into general notice and estimation, mainly owing to the excellent manner in which their natural capacities had been directed by the distinguished and successful talents of their tutor.

The affectionate interest manifested by Dr. Butler in the welfare of his pupils remained nearest to his heart to the last.* And in retiring from the duties of his scholastic station, in 1836, it appeared as his greatest comfort and happiness to find that St. John's College had given a good earnest of its intention to uphold the character of the school over which he had so long and so zealously presided, by the selection of the Rev. Benjamin Hall Kennedy as his successor, an appointment (it will be admitted by all) the most conducive to the future prosperity of the school, and consequently beneficial to the town and neighbourhood ; inasmuch as it is stamped upon high and indubitable authority that Mr. Kennedy is one of the most brilliant scholars which the learned editor of Æschylus ever sent forth,—the brightest star in that galaxy of distinguished pupils whose names adorn the boards of Shrewsbury school ; while from his experience of Dr. Butler's system, both as a pupil and assistant master in this seminary,—his subsequent

K 3

* The scholars, in grateful remembrance of the kindness of their preceptor, presented him (on his taking leave of the School, June 7th, 1836,) with a massive silver candelabrum, of three hundred guineas value, raised by their united contributions,—the subject a vine branch with Genii pressing the fruit, and bearing an appropriate inscription ; in acknowledging which Dr. Butler said, " under your future head master and his able coadjutor (the Rev. G. I. Welldon), and my long-tried and much-valued friends, the assistant masters, may you pursue your career with the same success as those who have gone before you ; and to my best wishes for your welfare and happiness, let me add, as my last official words, " FLOREAT SALOPIA !"

practice as a lecturer and private tutor at College, and as an assistant master for upwards of six years at Harrow, as well as from his own unrivalled talents and high literary distinctions,—from his fine taste and sound learning,—there is not a shadow of doubt but that he will fully maintain the reputation Shrewsbury School has already acquired.

The following annual prizes are distributed—

Pelham Prizes..........	Latin Verse	20 guineas.
	Greek Iambics............	10 guineas.
Trustees' Prize..........	Latin Essay	20 guineas.
Assistant Master's Prize ...	Latin Translation	10 guineas.
Head Master's Prizes	For the First and Second in the Examination	Books.

In 1832 this ancient and royal foundation was visited by three members of the royal family within two months : by his Royal Highness the Duke of Sussex, Sept. 5th ; by their Royal Highnesses the Duchess of Kent and the Princess Victoria, Nov. 1st.

THE SCHOOLS

are situate near the Castle, and display a handsome spacious structure of free-stone, built in the incongruous but fashionable style of architecture which prevailed in the 16th and 17th century ; wherein the Grecian and pointed arches are fantastically mixed together. The building occupies two sides of a quadrangle, with a square pinnacled tower at the angle, partly rebuilt in 1831.

The original school-room was of timber, to which the tower, chapel, and library were added in 1595. In the year 1630 the wooden portion was removed, and its site occupied by the present edifice, in the centre of which is a gateway, having a Corinthian column on each side, upon which are statues of a scholar and a graduate, bareheaded, in the dress of the times. Above the arch is a Greek inscription from Isocrates, which implies that a love of literature is necessary to the formation of a scholar. Over this are the armorial bearings of Charles the First.

The upper story of this part is occupied by the principal school-room, an apartment 82 feet by 21, and in the basement is the head master's school, in which are several panels containing the names of gentlemen educated here, and who have subsequently distinguished themselves at the Universities.* The upper moulding of each panel contains one of the following lines:—

TV . FACITO . MOX . CVM . MATVRA . ADOLEVERIT . AETAS
SIS . MEMOR . ATQVE . ANIMO . REPETAS . EXEMPLA . TVORVM
ET . TVA . TE . VIRTVS . MAGNA . INTER . PRAEMIA . DVCET.

The chapel forms the other wing of the building, and was consecrated Sept. 10th, 1617, when a sermon was preached on the occasion by Sampson Price, D. D. Chaplain in Ordinary to the King, from John x. 22, 23. It is 62 ft. long by 22 ft. wide, and contains a handsome pulpit and bible stand, and is separated from the ante-chapel by a carved skreen, displaying a series of interlaced arches resting on fluted Corinthian columns. Prayers are read here twice on school days.

Above the chapel, and of the same size, is the library, a noble room, rebuilt in 1815. The ceiling is richly adorned, and panelled into Gothic and ornamental compartments, on which are displayed the armorial bearings of the first and subsequent trustees. It contains a valuable collection of printed books and manuscripts, one side being occupied by the library of the late Dr. Taylor, editor of Demosthenes. Among the portraits which decorate the

* Of the one hundred and twenty first-rate honours recorded here, the present learned head master (Dr. Kennedy) claims more than one-twelfth for his own individual share.

walls of this elegant apartment are those of the Bishop of
Lichfield (late head master), the Reverends John Lloyd
and Leonard Hotchkiss (formerly masters), Queen Elizabeth, King Henry VIII. Edward VI. (the Founder), Locke,
Judge Jefferies, &c. &c.

At the south end of the room are four sepulchral stones
found at Wroxeter, near this town, three of which are fully
described by Pennant, in his North Wales. A small museum likewise contains other Roman antiquities from the
same place, with fossils and other curiosities.

The windows are embellished with escutcheons of the
arms of Edward VI. Queen Elizabeth, St. John's College,
Cambridge, the See of Lichfield, and the town, in stained
glass.

In front and at the back of the schools is a spacious
area, used as a promenade or play-ground for the scholars ;
contiguous to which are houses for the head, second, and
assistant masters, and ample halls for the accommodation
of boarders, who are numerous, and from all parts of the
kingdom.

Several exhibitions of £70 and £80 a-year belong to
this school, to which the freemen's sons are entitled for a
certain number of years. At a meeting of the trustees, held
23d May, 1836, it was resolved, in order more fully to
testify their own sense, and to perpetuate the memory, of
the unremitting assiduity and eminent ability with which
Dr. Butler has performed the duties of head-master of this
school for a period of thirty-eight years, restoring and augmenting by his energy and learning the utility and celebrity
of this ancient and royal foundation, to found an additional
exhibition of £100 per annum, to be called for ever " DR.
BUTLER'S EXHIBITION," and to be tenable by the sons of
freemen entering at either University.

LOCAL GOVERNMENT, CHARTERS, &c.

SHREWSBURY has received a succession of thirty-two royal charters from the time of King William the First to the first year of the reign of James the Second. The earliest charter preserved in the corporation archives is dated Nov. 11, 1189, being the first year of King Richard the First, which recites that a previous corporation had existed.

The last governing charter of the town was granted the 16th of June, 1639, by Charles the First.

The component parts of the corporation were a mayor, recorder, steward, common clerk, twenty-four aldermen, forty-eight assistants or common councilmen, two chamberlains, sword-bearer, serjeants at mace, &c.

The mayor was elected annually by the majority of aldermen and assistants, in council assembled, on the first Friday after the feast of St. Bartholomew, and sworn into office the first Friday after Michaelmas-day. Robert Burton, jun. Esq. was the last mayor chosen under the old charter.

The aldermen were elected by the mayor and aldermen from the assistants, and the latter from the burgesses at large.

Burgesses obtained their freedom by descent, or birth, or by serving a bona fide apprenticeship of seven years within the ancient limits of the borough to a freeman of one of the ancient incorporated companies.

According to the Municipal Act, which received the royal assent in 1835, the town was divided into five wards.*

On the 26th of December, 1835, each of the wards returned six members to form the new Town Council, who elected to their number, on the 31st, ten aldermen, which constitutes the municipal body of the town, from whom William Hazledine, Esq. was elected Mayor. To assist in the local government, the Secretary of State has subsequently appointed eight magistrates. Under the provisions of the above cited act, the annual election of mayor is fixed for the 9th of November.

The ancient COMMON SEAL of the municipal body is very curious, representing a view of the town,—its churches, domestic habitations, fortified gates and walls, beneath which the river is seen flowing under a bridge; above the latter is a shield bearing the arms of England, and on each side are similar shields charged with the cross of St. George and the town arms,—Azure, three leopard's faces Or. The inscription round this seal is—Sigillu . commune . libertatis . ville . Salopesburie . factu . ano . gre . m cccc xxv.

SESSIONS.

A petty sessions is held every Tuesday, and the mayor or some of the magistrates sit most days for the determination of minor offences.

A general court of QUARTER SESSIONS and gaol delivery for the town and liberties is held by the recorder, John Bather, Esq. on the Wednesday after the county sessions.

* The old liberties of the borough extended a few miles round Shrewsbury. A large part of this ancient boundary, possessing a property of the annual value of fifty thousand pounds, and which formerly used to contribute to the rates levied in connexion with the town, is now taken from the liberties and annexed to the county.

COURT OF RECORD.

This town possesses the privilege of a court of record, where actions for debt (to any amount) and ejectment within the liberties, can be brought. Judgment in a suit may be obtained in about six weeks, if the defendant pleads the general issue.

COURT OF REQUESTS.

Small debts exceeding two shillings and under forty shillings, are taken cognizance of by a Court of Requests, established in 1783. The court meets every other Wednesday in the Town Hall, the commissioners of which must be resident within the town, and possessed of freehold property of thirty pounds per annum value, or a clear personal estate of £600 value.

MEMBERS OF PARLIAMENT.

This town is a borough by prescription, and has sent two members to parliament from the earliest assembling of that body. Previous to the general reform act the right of election was in the burgesses inhabiting within the ancient borough, paying scot and lot, and not receiving alms or charity. The elective franchise is now extended to £10 householders resident within the boundaries settled by act of parliament, July 15, 1832.

TRADING COMPANIES.

From a remote period several incorporated trading companies existed here,* who exacted fines from what were termed " foreigners ;" that is, individuals who had not served an apprenticeship to a freeman, or who were not

---

* A merchant guild is supposed to have been established as a voluntary association as early as the year 1128 ; for, among other customs granted by Henry III. there was one by which no person who was not a member of the " merchant guild" could exercise merchandize in the borough without the consent of the burgesses.

the eldest sons of freemen, if they commenced business in the " craft or calling" of any of these guilds; the chief of which were the Drapers and Mercers: the former possessed a considerable property, and were incorporated by Edward the Fourth, as were the latter in 1480 by the same king. The Barber Chirurgeons were chartered by Edward the First in 1304, and incorporated by James II. in 1686, with the Wax and Tallow Chandlers. The charter of the com-brethren of Painters, Booksellers, &c. is dated May 8th, 19th of Edward IV. The Builders, &c. 19th Q. Elizabeth, 1577. The composition of the Tailors, 1627, and recites a more ancient grant. The Smiths, Armourers, &c. have a composition, 19th James I. 1621. That of the Shoe-makers is the most recent, being dated 1739. The Butchers have lost their charter, money, and records; and several other " crafts" have only left a name behind.

These fraternities comprehend in their incorporation many more trades than have been specified. Their utility in the infancy of commerce, as so many brotherhoods for the protection of different trading interests, is evident; but having survived the original purpose of institution, their advantage had been long questioned, and the powers which they possessed became defunct under the recent Municipal Bill. It is not, however, too much to suppose but they might, as SOCIAL BODIES, still effect many good purposes, not the least of which would be the aggregation of brotherly feeling and good fellowship.

SHREWSBURY SHOW.

This annual pageant is perhaps, with the exception of Coventry, the only one of the kind in the kingdom. It originated in the celebration of the splendid festival of Corpus Christi in the church of Rome, which was observed with much pomp and solemnity by the masters and wardens of the different trading companies, the members of the corporation, the parochial clergy, and the religious fraternities of the town.

The procession, so far back as the 27th of Henry VI. appears to have been " tyme owt of mynde." and which several of the guilds were obliged to support. This is apparent from their " compositions," or bye-laws, containing regulations to that effect. That of the Weavers (anno 1444) provides, that certain fines shall be applied to the " sustentacon and encreece of the lyght of the seyd crafte " of Wev's, at the feast of Corpus Xp'i daye." The composition of the Mercers, Ironmongers, and Goldsmiths directs that they shall provide " 300 mede of wax yearly, to " be burnt in the p'cession of the feast of Corpus Xp'i."

After the Reformation, the religious part of the ceremony was set aside, and as a substitute the second Monday after Trinity Sunday adopted as a day of recreation and feasting on Kingsland, where each company had a small enclosure, within which is a building called an " arbour," surrounded by trees, and where refreshment was accustomed to be liberally provided by the respective trades. Only seven of the arbours now remain, each of which had formerly the arms of the company carved or painted over the entrance.

The anniversary has often been anticipated by Salopians with feelings of delight,—as affording an annual treat of hospitality and good cheer. The town on the occasion has presented an appearance of lively interest, conducive also to its trade; the bells of the different churches sent forth their melodious and enlivening peals, while the incorporated companies were passing to their places of muster; at noon they assembled together at the Castle, from whence they proceeded through the streets to Kingsland, accompanied by their respective flags, banners, and music of all kinds, most of the companies having some character dressed in personification of a king, or emblematical of their respective crafts, and followed by a goodly array of com-brethren walking (as it were) hand in hand together. The mayor and his friends followed afterwards on horseback, and were wont to be entertained by the trading companies with a dejeune in each arbour.

Such was " Shrewsbury Show." An attempt was made in 1823 to revive the ancient pageantry; but during the last few years there has been a sad falling off in the display, and it is to be feared that the manifold changes of the present times, and the refined dispositions (probably) of some modern minds, are causes that will soon hasten to a discontinuance what remains of this ancient custom and lively picture of old English manners.[*]

The following extract from a scarce poem published in the year 1770, entitled " Shrewsbury Quarry," is probably the only authentic account which will afford some idea of the " Show" at that period :—

> What friendly forms in social pomp draw near,
> With thankful smiles to bless the bounteous year!
> In glad procession, brotherhood, and bloom,
> (Like *Flora*'s festals near thy walls, oh Rome,)

---

[*] A more extended account of this pageant, by the author of " Memorials of Shrewsbury," will be found in the Gentleman's Magazine for July, 1833.

The bands distinguished, yet harmonious move,
Their ensigns concord, and their leaders love;
To KINGSLAND's Arbours once a year they go,
In ordered elegance serene and slow;
The Bodies Corporate in classes bright—
In different classes, but in one delight;
There blend with mutual hands the friendly bowls,
There blend their wishes and there blend their souls;
The yearly *Archon** over all presides,
Their state he governs, and their joy he guides,
There mixing jovial with each jovial band,
To each he gives his heart—to each his hand;
With each he quaffs the invigorating cheer,
To friendship sacred, and the hallow'd year;
There union, brotherhood, and mirth combine,
In every face these vital virtues shine.
The sun would gladly in his course delay,
And stretch beyond its lengthened bound the day,
To gaze with rapture, as each bosom glows,
On these rich blessings which his beam bestows;
His prone career, his cadence they behold,
His western stage in crimson clad, and gold,
They see his orb reluctant now go down,
Then march in happy order back to town;
There polish'd pleasures teem with new delight,
And balls and banquets crown the genial night.

* Mayor.

THE COUNTY HALL.

Architectural excellence has been said to consist in the judicious and skilful adaptation of an edifice to its specific destination, and in the appropriate and tasteful display of its interior and exterior ornaments, and that public buildings should be distinguished by decisive and apposite characteristic features of their purpose. How far this has been exemplified in the Salop County Hall, the foregoing illustrative vignette will in a great measure decide. The design is by Sir Robert Smirke, and the style Italian; the main feature of the elevation being a bold cornice resting on sculptured modillons.

The principal front is divided into three divisions by projecting string courses, and is 112½ feet in length; the portion facing High-street, 58 feet; height to the top of parapet 54 feet.

On examining the interior of the structure, it will be evident that the architect has made the most of a very limited space of ground: the different apartments are convenient, lofty, and well adapted to the various purposes for which they are intended. The offices in particular, although plain, are fitted up in a most substantial manner.

The entrance hall is 22 feet 8 inches by 21½ feet, having on the right a lobby leading to the crown court, and a room for the use of witnesses waiting for examination in that court. On the left is a similar entrance to the nisi prius court, and the mayor's room (appropriated to counsel during the assizes). Opposite the entrance door is the grand staircase, spacious and of easy ascent; on the first landing are three doorways, the centre one leading to the judges' retiring room (which communicates with the courts), and those on either hand to the magisterial bench in the respective courts, which are of equal dimensions, 42 feet by 36 feet.*

The accommodation for the gentlemen of the bar was intended to have been similar to that provided (under the direction of the same architect) in the Court of King's Bench and several other places; but objections being made by the counsel on this circuit, and a petition sent to the magistrates, this arrangement was altered, and the space immediately before the judge is occupied by a large table, with sufficient seats for twenty counsellors, having a row of seats behind for attornies.

The bench is elevated $3\frac{1}{2}$ feet above the floor, on each side of which is accommodation for the magistrates.

The ceiling of both courts is panelled and ornamented. and the walls are lined with wood as high as the small side galleries, which are intended for the use of the grand and special jurors.

In each court is a gallery for the public, the two front benches of which are partitioned off for jurymen in waiting. To these galleries are separate entrances from the principal front, in order to prevent the annoyance of a crowd in the vestibule of the hall, through which admittance will be afforded for those persons who have business in the courts.

Under the public galleries are lock-up rooms for the jury.

The nisi prius court is lighted by a lantern, which occupies a considerable space in the ceiling; and beneath the public gallery of this court is the waiting-room for witnesses. The first story is approached by a broad flight of stairs: on the left is the grand jury room, 30 feet by 18 feet, lofty and finished in a tasteful manner, having a communication with the gallery in the crown court for the presentment of bills. Attached to this apartment is a large room for witnesses

* The former courts were 44 ft. 9 in. by 31 ft.

attending the grand jury; the floor is of stone, and forms the ceiling of the entrance hall. To the right is the office of the clerk of indictments.

From this division of the building the staircase leads to the entrance of the GREAT ROOM, adapted for a third court or other public purposes requiring space. It is decorated with an enriched cornice and panelled ceiling; the dimensions are 45½ feet by 32½ feet, and 19 feet high, having a recess at one end; it is lighted by windows at the side and back, and is well ventilated by means of tubes which pass from the ceiling through the roof.

By another ascent of steps the upper floor is gained. To the left are offices for the clerk of the peace, with a fire-proof room as a depositary for records. Similar rooms to the right are appropriated for the town clerk.

In the rear of the building is a house for the hall-keeper, resting over an entrance intended as a passage for the cart conveying prisoners from the gaol, where they are set down in an area having stairs leading to spacious and airy cells; these, with cellars for other purposes, occupy a considerable portion of the base of the building, which stands upon a concrete foundation, 10 feet thick, rendered necessary (from the insufficient state of the ground) to support the weight of a massive structure. In excavating for this purpose, many curiosities were found; and although the required depth was 19 feet below the level of the street, the natural strata was not discovered, the whole bed being a complete bog of peaty soil of unequal depth,—a sufficient cause for all the fissures visible for several years past in the external and internal walls of the former fabric, which was only completed in 1785, at a cost of £11,000.

In 1832, Thomas Telford, Esq. was requested to examine the nature of the foundations, when it appeared that the oak sapling piles, or rather stakes, on which the building rested were totally decayed, and become as soft as the earth by which they were surrounded. To restore the walls to a sound state was deemed a difficult and expensive undertaking, even if practicable. A new building was therefore determined upon, Sir Robert Smirke having guaranteed a sufficient foundation on the old site, by taking out the whole of the soil, and replacing it by an artificial body of concrete. His plan was adopted by the county magistrates, Jan. 28th, 1834, and in the month of April workmen commenced taking down the old edifice,* and the new building progressed towards completion so as to be ready by March, 1837.

The foundations appear to have succeeded beyond the expectations of all concerned, and the building does great credit to the contractors, Messrs. Birch and Sons. The estimated cost is about £12,000, raised by a county rate.

THE GUILD HALL AND EXCHEQUER

of the town is incorporated with the county hall, by an arrangement with the county previous to the erection of the late edifice.

The following portraits, presented to the late corporation, will decorate the walls of the new building:—King Charles I. Charles II. William III. George I. George II. George III. Queen Charlotte, Admiral Benbow (a native of Shrewsbury), the Right Hon. Lord Hill (by Sir William Beechy), and Admiral Owen (by R. Evans, Esq. a townsman). The two latter portraits possess life and spirit in their execution; and are justly esteemed most faithful resemblances of these illustrious heroes and fellow-citizens.

---

* This structure was 111 feet by 51 ; its exterior feature was a bold pediment, supported by four three-quarter columns of the Ionic order,

THE MARKET HOUSE

is a spacious building, unequalled in point of ornamental decoration by any similar structure in the kingdom. It not only gives a most prominent feature to the area in front of the county hall, but is a general and interesting object of attraction to strangers.

The principal front is to the west, over the portal of which are the arms of Queen Elizabeth in high relief, and the date 1596. On each side of this portal is an open arcade, consisting of three round arches, which form the main building; above these is a series of square mullioned windows, surmounted by a rich fanciful parapet consisting of curved embrasures, which rise at certain distances into a kind of pinnacle.

Above the northern arch is the following inscription, having on one side the arms of France and England quarterly, and on the other those of the town :—

> The xvth day of June was this building begun,
> William Jones and Thomas Charlton, Gent. then
> Bailiffs, and was erected and covered in their time.
>
> 1595.

Immediately over this is a tabernacled niche, containing a fine statue of RICHARD DUKE OF YORK, in complete armour; one hand is supported on his breast, and the other pointing below to a device of three roses carved on a stalk. A tablet corresponding with the town arms, finely sculptured in relief, on the left hand of the figure, records its removal from the tower on the Welsh bridge, in 1791. In the same situation on the corresponding end of the hall is the figure of an angel in a canopied niche, bearing a shield of the arms of France and England quarterly. This originally stood within the chamber of the Gate Tower at the Castle Gates, from whence it was preserved when the remaining portion of that ancient barrier gave way to modern houses in 1825.

The basement of the Market House is 105 feet long by 24 feet wide, and is used on Saturdays as the corn-market; at other times it forms an useful promenade, especially in wet weather.

The inscription on the north end has often excited surprise, how so large and ornamental a building could have been completed within a period of less than four months. The nature of the case would seem, that the stone-work and timber-framing had perhaps previously been wrought, so that no time might be lost, and the utmost endeavours used, in the re-edification of a building which was almost indispensible at that period,—when corn was for the most part brought to market in the *bulk*, and not sold by *sample* as in the present day. This conjecture is somewhat confirmed by the following extract from a manuscript chronicle in the possession of the writer:—

" 1595. In the month of January this year the old building in the Corn Market Place was agreed to be taken down, and the timber-work thereof was sold, and another with all speed was to be erected with stone and timber in the same place, and a sumptuous hall aloft, with a spacious market house below for corn was begun, the foundation and fencing whereof was a quarter of a year before it was finished, and the stone work was begun upon the 15th day of June following, and was finished and almost covered in before the bailiffs of the said year went out of their office the Michaelmas following."

THE BRIDGES.

Two handsome stone bridges cross the river Severn nearly in a parallel direction. These were preceded by very ancient structures, defended by embattled towers, and were excellent specimens of the fortified bridges necessary in former times for the protection of the town. Being extremely narrow and dilapidated, they were taken down in the last century; a brief notice, therefore, of their ancient state will be sufficient.

THE OLD WELSH BRIDGE

was considered as the chief architectural ornament of the town, consisting of seven arches, and situated a few yards higher up the stream than the present structure. Its gates and towers at each end were of the finest kind of castellated building, being richly decorated with shields and sculpture ; and their demolition is much to be regretted.

Above one of the gates stood the armed statue of a knight, which was removed in 1791, and placed in a niche on the front of the Market House. This effigy was an important object of attraction to the Welshmen in passing through the gate, from a tradition retained by them even to modern times, that it represented Llewelyn Prince of Wales, or David, the last of the British Princes, whom Roger Coke facetiously calls " King Taffy," but which recent antiquaries have, from its attendant embellishments, more properly assigned to Richard Duke of York, father of Edward IV.

THE OLD EAST OR STONE BRIDGE

consisted rather of two bridges (being divided by an island of 118 feet broad), extending 864 feet in length, and comprising seventeen arches. The thoroughfare over it in the widest part was only twelve feet, being impeded by a range of thirty-three houses disposed on each side, after the manner of London Bridge in former times.

The further bridge from the town had eleven arches, and was properly denominated " THE ABBEY BRIDGE," for it extended to the precinct of the monastery, and passed over none of the water of the Severn except in times of flood, receiving only a small portion of a rivulet called Meole Brook, the channel of which is still visible in the meadows opposite the Council House.

The narrow state of this bridge having been long matter of complaint and inconvenience, a subscription was commenced in 1765 to widen it, towards which Sir John Astley, Bart. gave £1000.

The expediency of the undertaking was so apparent, from the liberal subscriptions which came in from all parts of the county, that encouragement was given to erect an entire new bridge, from a design furnished by Mr. John Gwynn, architect, of London, and a native of Shrewsbury. The first stone of the bridge was laid June 29th, 1769, by the munificent promoter of the undertaking, Sir John Astley, Bart; and the work was so far completed as to afford a passage (March 14th, 1774) for the High Sheriff, John Owen, Esq. of Woodhouse, and a numerous body of gentlemen on horseback who accompanied him to meet the judges of assize, whom they escorted into town over the new bridge, since styled

THE ENGLISH BRIDGE,

which is a most substantial structure, 410 ft. in length, and composed of seven arches, crowned by a bold balustrade; the primary object in its construction was to contrive as much space as possible for the water during floods, to accomplish which, the central arch (60 feet in diameter) was raised double the height of the end arches, an elevation perhaps not accordant with or agreeable to later opinions of ease and convenience. With the exception of this defect, its elegance and beauty of architecture is probably surpassed by few bridges in the kingdom, and is in every respect an ornament to the town, and an equally noble monument of the public spirit and generosity of the gentry of the county, who so laudably exerted themselves to further its erection.

The ornamental parts, though sparingly are yet tastefully disposed. The keystone of the central arch on the north side is adorned with a fine head of SABRINA, " goddess of the river," while that on the opposite side bears a spirited head of NEPTUNE, the " father of fountains." On the piers of this arch rest finely carved dolphins. The keystones of the other arches are worked into a shell. The parapet of the bridge rises into a pediment, in the centre of which (on each side facing the river) is the town arms, and the date of the completion of the bridge, MDCCLXXIV.

The total cost, including the purchase of the houses which stood on and near the bridge, acts of parliament, &c. was £15,710. 3s. 3d.

LORD HILL'S COLUMN.

LORD HILL'S COLUMN.

This noble column, erected in honour of the VALOUR and VIRTUES of an individual whose well-earned laurels have gained him a firm affection in the hearts of his countrymen, and truly rendered him SALOPIA'S PRIDE and ENGLAND'S GLORY, stands on a rising ground at the entrance of the town from the London road, and forms an interesting object to the surrounding country. It is said to be the largest Grecian Doric column in the world.

The first stone was laid by the Salopian Lodge of Free and Accepted Masons, on the 27th December, 1814.

The pedestal is square, rising upon two steps, with a large pier at each angle, on which are placed lions couchant, worked out of Grinshill stone by Mr. Carline, of this town.

The diameter at the base is 15 feet, and the other dimensions are as follow :—

	ft.	in.
Height of the pedestal	13	6
Shaft and capital	91	6
Pedestal for the figure	11	6
Statue of his lordship.................	17	0
Total height............	133	6

The colossal statue of his Lordship on the summit is executed in artificial stone by Messrs. Coade and Sealy, of London, modelled by Panzetta. The original design for the column was by Mr. Haycock, of Shrewsbury.

The contractors were Messrs. Simpson and Lawrence; on the death of the former, the work devolved upon Mr. Straphen, who completed it, and erected the elegant staircase within the building at his own expense.

The last stone was laid in 1816, on the anniversary of the memorable battle of Waterloo.

On the pedestal are the following inscriptions :

ON THE SOUTH SIDE.

Civi . svo . Rolando

Domino . Baroni . Hill . ab . Almarez . et . Hawkstone
Popvlares . eivs . ex . agro . atqve . municipio . Salopiensi
Colvmnam . hancce . cvm . statva . P . C.

A . S . MDCCCXVI.

Is . in . re . militari . qvemadmodvm . se . gesserit
Testes . sint . Lvsitania . Hispania . Galliae
Narbonensis . ac . Belgica
Artvrivs . Dvx . a . Wellington
Sociorvm . et . qvidem . hostivm . exercitvs.

ON THE NORTH SIDE.

To Lieutenant General Rowland Lord Hill,
Baron Hill of Almarez and Hawkstone, G. C. B.
Not more distinguished for his skill and courage in the field,
During the arduous campaigns in Spain and Portugal,
The South of France, and the memorable Plains of Waterloo,
Than for his benevolent and paternal care,
In providing for the comforts and supplying the necessities
Of his victorious countrymen,
And for that humanity and generosity
Which their vanquished foes experienced and acknowledged :
The inhabitants of the Town and County of Salop
Have erected this Column and Statue,
As a memorial of their respect and gratitude to an illustrious
contemporary,
And an incitement to emulation in the heroes and
patriots of future ages.
A. D. MDCCCXVI.

ON THE EAST SIDE.

Roleia	Arroyo del Molinos	Hillette
Vimiera	Almarez	Orthes
Corunna	Vittoria	Aire
Douro	Pyrenees	Tarbes
Talavera	Nive	Toulouse
Busaco	Nivelle	Waterloo.

This splendid memorial is constructed of fine Grinshill stone; the total expence, including the cottage and other incidentals, amounted to £5973. 13s. 2d. which was raised by a subscription throughout the county.

Within the shaft is a staircase of 172 steps, forming a well in the centre, each step having an iron baluster with a gilt letter inserted on a small panel, which gives the following inscription:—

" This staircase was the gift of John Straphen, the builder, as his donation towards erecting this Column. The first stone of the foundation was laid December 27th, 1814, and completed June 18th, 1816, the anniversary of the glorious Battle of Waterloo."

The column may be ascended by a gratuity to the keeper, who resides in a neat Doric cottage adjoining.

From the railing at the top is a delightful panoramic view of the fertile plain of Shropshire, to which the bold appearance of Shrewsbury, and its once formidable Castle mantled with leafy verdure, forms a prominent contrast.

The surrounding distances are replete with interest, being composed of fine undulating hills and mountains. Proceeding northward, the eye ranges over the Nesscliff and Selattyn hills, the mountainous tract of the Berwyn, the luxuriantly crowned summit of Pimhill, the wild and romantic rock of Grinshill, and the gentler eminences of Hawkstone, whose tasteful plantations and noble woods are seen at a distance of twelve miles, among which rises the " Obelisk," erected to the memory of Sir Rowland Hill, the first Protestant Lord Mayor of London.

In the foreground north-east is the plain, renowned in history, and immortalized by Shakspeare in dramatic poetry, as the scene of the great and important Battle of Shrewsbury, in 1403, in commemoration of which King Henry IV. pi-

ously founded a church, called to this day " Battlefield,"
the well-proportioned tower of which is easily distinguished.

The turrets of the modern castellated mansion of Sundorne are particularly striking, and remind us of the beautiful lines of Mrs. Hemans—

> The stately Homes of England,
> How beautiful they stand!
> Amidst their tall ancestral trees,
> O'er all the pleasant land.

Further eastward are the venerable and truly picturesque
ruins of Haghmond Monastery, founded in the year 1100,
for canons of the order of St. Augustine.   Near the remains
of this once more noble pile is the wooded ascent of Haghmond Hill, and its conspicuously placed Shooting Tower,
beneath which is the retired village of Uffington and its
primitive church.

Direct east stands exalted in noble majesty the isolated
Wrekin, the *natural Heart of Shropshire,* in front of
which appears the exuberant foliage surrounding Longner
Hall.   Directing the eye southwards, is Charlton Hill,
bounded by the towering summit of the Brown Clee (1820
feet in height), and the Lawley, Acton Burnell Park, Fro-
desley, and other Shropshire hills, among which is the lofty
Caerdoc, otherwise Caer Caradoc, where Caractacus (the
last of the original British princes) is said to have displayed
his patriotism and daring spirit against the united efforts of
the Roman forces.

Onward in the horizon, beyond a remote cultivated
country, is the Longmynd with its straight outline, and the
Stiperstones, topped by rocks, similar to the august relics
of castellated grandeur; these are connected by the Brom-
low and Long Mountain; and the panorama terminates
with the lofty mountains of Breidden, Cefn y Cayster, and

Moelygolfa, which, with more distant eminences, form a fine back-ground to a portion of the town, while the middle distance all around is unequalled for richness and fertility.

Nor, whilst extolling the environs and distant scenes around, let us forget the immediate vicinity of the Column: its verdant pastures, sequestered lanes, stately trees, and rural scenery, are surpassed by none so near a populous county town.

THE TOWN AND COUNTY GAOL

Is situated on a dry, beautiful, and salubrious eminence, a short distance from the Castle.

The front of the prison displays rather a bold appearance, having two rusticated stone lodges and a gateway in the centre; over the latter is a bust of the philanthropic HOWARD, by Bacon.

The interior possesses every necessary convenience appropriate to its purpose that sagacity and humanity can devise. It is spacious, airy, and well supplied with water, by means of a pump worked by the prisoners.

The governor's house faces the gateway, and forms the southern front of the building. The chapel stands in the centre of the whole, and is lighted by a lantern surmounted by a gilt cross. It is octagonal, and contrived that while all the prisoners may see the clergyman, every class is so separated as to be hid from each other.

The prison is further divided into four principal courts, besides other smaller ones; these are surrounded by cloisters with groined arches; above these are the sleeping cells, the communication to which is by railed galleries. A due regard to the gradations of vice is strictly observed in

the classification of the prisoners, most of whom are occupied during the day in some little manufactory or useful
employment, by which habits of industry are acquired that
may protect them from temptations to plunder or miscon-
duct when released from confinement.

Executions take place on the roof of the porter's lodge.

The prison was begun in 1787, and completed (from a
plan by Mr. Haycock) in 1793, at an expense of about
£30,000. The entire building is surrounded by a strong
brick wall, flanked with rusticated stone buttresses.

THE BUTTER AND POULTRY MARKET,

on Pride-hill, was erected in 1819 by voluntary contributions
amounting to £2000. It is a building unworthy our town
and the ample produce brought to its weekly markets. In
1830 it was adjudged to be taken down as being unsuitable
and incommodious. A meeting was held to arrange for a
new building upon an improved plan, the money to be
raised by shares of £25 each, but circumstances prevented
this desirable undertaking, which is much to be regretted,
as complaints have long been made of the obstruction
in the thoroughfare (which is often attended with delay and
danger) on market and fair days, by persons exposing their
goods and marketables for sale in the street.

THE CIRCUS BUTTER & CHEESE MARKET,

from its situation near the Welsh Bridge, possesses superior
advantages for the conveyance of goods and general trade.
It was opened about the year 1822 by Mr. H. Newton.

THE NEW BUTTER AND CHEESE MARKET

Is an elegant and commodious edifice situated in Howard-street, Castle-foregate, and possesses every requisite convenience for the disposal of butter, cheese, and other agricultural produce, and merchandize.

The exterior consists of a centre and two wings, the centre forming the portico and principal entrance, which is decorated with two Grecian columns and entablature. The whole of the front is cemented, and possesses an unity of parts and a boldness of proportion unusual in buildings of this description.

The interior is divided into two stories, the lower or basement being vaulted with groined arches springing from brick piers, which afford an equality of height in almost every part. The entrance to the basement is on the north side, and (owing to the fall in the street) is of sufficient height to admit a waggon. The canal is on the south side, and nearly level with the floor of the basement, to which there is a communication, affording a ready transit for goods.

The upper or principal floor of the Market contains an area of 5400 feet; the roof is supported by four rows of iron pillars; the centre part being raised nine feet, has a range of windows on each side, by which a proper ventilation is obtained as well as additional light.

Attached to the upper end of the building is a second entrance, communicating with an office for the clerk of the market.

The first stone of the edifice was laid by Mr. W. H. Griffiths, May 28th, 1835, and was completed by that time in the next year, in a manner creditable to the architects, Messrs. FALLOWS and HART, of Birmingham.

THE SALOP INFIRMARY.

Among the various channels through which the stream of christian benevolence pursues its fertilizing course to the ocean of charity, those Institutions which have for their express design the cultivation of the mind and the alleviation of misfortunes which the casualties of life and the infirmities of human nature render mankind alike heir to, afford undoubtedly the safest application of real beneficence, being, in a measure, free from that imposition with which an indiscriminate charity has unfortunately so often to contend.

From the most remote period the virtuous breast has cultivated the sublime desire of mitigating, as far as possible, the pain and wretchedness consequent upon disease and suffering,—hence we find that the munificence which characterised our forefathers centuries ago was not altogether confined to the erection of numerous places for Divine Worship, and for which our town was early distinguished, but that the pleasing pain of sympathy prompted them also to build and endow " Hospitals" for the reception of the sick and diseased, and " Almshouses" for the aged and infirm. The first record we possess of the existence of such charitable institutions in Shrewsbury is as early as the time of Henry the Second, beside an " Infirmary" founded by Earl Roger de Montgomery, within the precinct of the " Abbey," as an asylum for diseased and superannuated monks, a fragment of which erection yet remains.

The rapacity, however, which disgraced the dissolution of Monasteries and whatever sustained the character of a " Religious House," has, with a solitary exception, rendered these ancient Hospitals defunct;—nor was it until the commencement of the last century that the attention of the public was particularly directed to the foundation of Hospitals or Infirmaries, and which, from the number of hospitals erected in the course of that period, will, no doubt, be a memorable age in the annals of Medical Charities ;— whilst it may be no mean compliment to our town and county to mention that its inhabitants early caught the rising spark of this generous flame, and had the distinguished honour of being the fifth in the kingdom to form the way in establishing a Provincial Asylum, on the basis of public benevolence,—THE SALOP INFIRMARY having commenced its salutary operations April 25th, 1747.

The building which preceded the present stately erection having been originally designed for a private residence, and although repeatedly enlarged and improved, being found to be insufficient for the accommodation of the additional number of patients consequent upon an increasing population, as well as inconvenient in many respects for the purpose it was designed to fulfil, it was resolved, at a meeting held Nov. 16, 1826, that a new Infirmary should be built on the site of the old one, at the estimated cost of about £16,000. As there was, however, much disinclination on the part of the subscribers present to take so large a sum from the funds of the institution, a considerable portion of which, having been bequeathed for its *support*, was therefore deemed sacred, a subscription was resolved upon and commenced immediately, when no less than £4,666 was subscribed by the noblemen and gentlemen then present,—a truly noble example of SALOPIAN GENEROSITY.

In the month of April, 1827, the patients were removed to a temporary infirmary, arranged in the Shrewsbury House of Industry; upon which workmen immediately commenced taking down the old building, and with such speed that on the 19th of July, the anniversary of our late revered monarch's coronation, the ceremony of laying the first stone of the new structure was performed by the Right Hon. Lord Hill, assisted by the late Venerable Archdeacon Owen, some of the committee, with the contractors and surveyor.

The building thus auspiciously begun, proceeded rapidly to a completion so as to be opened on September 16, 1830. It is of free-stone, and of a plain Grecian character in design, 170 feet long by 80 feet high, having a Doric portico in the centre, the ends projecting with pilasters at each angle. At the top of the building, on a tablet, is the following inscription :—

SALOP INFIRMARY,

Established 1745,

Supported by Voluntary Subscriptions and Benefactions.

REBUILT 1830.

The interior comprises four stories; in the basement story the offices, to the number of twenty-two, are well arranged, having a convenient court for coal, &c. and water

N

supplied to the several apartments. The principal floor is appropriated to the board room, dispensary, waiting room for the patients, and admitting rooms for the faculty, with private apartments for the house-surgeon and matron, and two wards for surgical cases.

The first floor is for male patients, and consists of seven wards, with a day-room, scullery, and bath rooms: the upper floor, for female patients, has the same accommodation, with the addition of a large and lofty operation room, enclosed by two pair of folding doors, having wards on each side; in the attics are four other wards, with nurses' rooms, &c. The ascent to these apartments is by staircases situated at each end of the building, connected by spacious galleries, which afford the means of free ventilation.

In addition to the conveniences with which this elegant structure is replete, the *patent hot-water apparatus*, erected for the purpose of warming the Infirmary, must not be overlooked. The apparatus consists of a boiler, placed in the basement floor of the building, from which, by means of a pipe rising from its top, the water heated therein is conveyed to the highest level required, from whence it descends (in its passage to the boiler) to what are called the water stoves, situated in the several galleries. By this mode of heating the several apartments, opportunity is afforded not only of having a supply of hot water to each scullery, bath, and floor, but nightly attendance to the fire is rendered altogether unnecessary.

Whilst the interior accommodations of the Infirmary are highly conducive to the health and comfort of the inmates, the external arrangements are so constructed that such of the patients as are able may possess every benefit resulting from exercise and pure air, a spacious terrace having been constructed, and extending beyond the length of the eastern front, from which a most expansive and interesting view presents itself. In short, the whole of the arrangements of the new Salop Infirmary are admirably adapted for the purpose they are designed to fulfil, and whilst the workmanship, the materials, and general construction are of the best description, and reflect the highest credit on the several contractors, the building it is to be desired will, from its site and general formation, remain a lasting monument not only of Salopian liberality, but of general usefulness.

The building was designed by Messrs. Haycock, of this town, and the total expence of its erection was £18,735. 18s. 10d. of which sum £13,044. 1s. 3d. was raised by public subscriptions and collections, the balance being made up by the sale of a part of the capital stock of the institution. The Infirmary is liberally supported by subscriptions and benefactions. From its establishment to Midsummer, 1835, the sum of £164,220. 11s. 3d. has been received for its support; 44,058 in-patients admitted, and 72,328 out-patients recommended as fit objects for its benefits.

The average annual expence is about £2230, and the weekly number of patients in the house 82; and 2429 out-patients were relieved in 1835.

A treasurer is annually chosen, and the affairs of the house are managed by eight directors, assisted by a secretary. The directors are chosen from the trustees, who are subscribers of two guineas and upwards per annum, of whom four retire from their office half-yearly.

The domestic arrangements are under the care of a matron; and a surgeon with a salary is resident in the house, so that medical aid may be always at hand.

The medical officers of the establishment gratuitously devote their time and apply their skill in promoting the benevolent design of the institution.

The clergy of the town officiate by turns weekly as chaplains to the house. And two weekly visitors from the resident subscribers go round the wards, by which the patients have an opportunity of stating any dissatisfaction that may exist, and having it reported to the board of directors, who assemble every Saturday morning for the dispatch of the ordinary business of the charity and the admission and discharge of patients.

Every patient must be recommended by a subscriber, except in the case of casualties.

The anniversary meeting is held in the Hunt week; when a numerous assemblage of noblemen and gentlemen accompany the treasurer from the Infirmary to St. Chad's church, where a sermon is preached and a collection made in aid of its funds, which always produces a sum truly honourable to the county.

Several tables of legacies and benefactions for the support of the Infirmary are fixed on the walls of the board room; and the cornice is adorned with a series of armorial bearings of all the noblemen and gentlemen who have filled the office of treasurer to the institution.

An auxiliary fund is attached to the hospital, for the purpose of assisting convalescent in-patients in returning to their homes.

EYE AND EAR DISPENSARY.

It would be superfluous to offer any observations on the importance of the two senses of Vision and Hearing, or on the prevalence of the various disorders to which the organs of those senses are liable; and whilst a general resource has been provided for the poor in the noble institution just noticed, for such diseases and accidents as they might be afflicted with, it has been thought expedient to form separate institutions for the relief of such disorders or defects in the human frame as are found more prevalent; since by directing medical and surgical skill to one particular object, efficient results may be the more easily obtained. To further this design, the Shropshire Eye and Ear Dispensary was established in 1818. During seventeen years of its progress 3583 patients have been admitted, and, as among these several have been restored to the blessing of sight, the institution is deserving of public support.

The dispensary is held in Castle-street, under the care of a surgeon. Annual subscribers of one guinea have, according to the original resolution, the right of recommending two patients within the year; but this is not in all cases strictly adhered to.

ST. GILES'S HOSPITAL,

it is considered, was originally established for the reception of persons afflicted with leprosy—a disease much more common among the ancients and in warmer climates than in Europe, into which it is said to have been introduced by the Crusaders in the time of Henry the First. King Henry tha Second, if not the founder of this hospital, granted to it 30s. yearly (equal to £80 of modern currency) of the rent which he received from the sheriff of Shropshire for the county, towards the support of the infirm or diseased occupants, as well as a small toll upon all corn and flour exposed to sale in Shrewsbury, either on market days or otherwise. The original grant of money is still paid by the sheriff to the Earl of Tankerville, who, as " Master of the Hospital," and holding certain lands for its maintenance, nominates four hospitallers, who have each a comfortable

house and garden, adjoining St. Giles's church-yard, with
one shilling and sixpence weekly, a small allowance for
coal, and clothing annually.

ST JOHN'S HOSPITAL,

although an asylum " for honest poverty and old age," did
not escape the rapacity which characterised the dissolution
of religious houses.   It stood in the suburb of Frankwell,
near a place since called The Stew.   Speed notices its site
in his map (1610); but not a fragment of the building now
remains.

THE DRAPERS' ALMSHOUSES.

The generally received opinion has been that these
almshouses were founded, in 1461, by Degory Watur,
Draper, from the circumstance that he lived himself in the
centre house, or " almshouse hall," among the poor people,
and whose practice (as a Manuscript Chronicle records) was
to attend them " dailye to our Lady's Chirch, and to kneel
with them in a long pew in the quire made for them and
himself."

The ancient records, however, of the Drapers' Company show that a building and endowment of almshouses by that company for poor people existed long previous to the foundation attributed to Degory Watur, who seems to have been only the founder in so far as their re-erection took place, under his management, during his wardenship or stewardship of the company, of which he was a member.

The old almshouses extended along the whole of the west side of St. Mary's church-yard: and, being much dilapidated and very incommodious dwellings, they were taken down in 1825. The present building, completed in the above year, from a design by Mr. J. Carline, now consists of eighteen comfortable habitations, of two chambers each; the front is in the old English style of architecture, having in the centre a gateway within an embattled tower; in the centre of the latter are the armorial bearings of the Drapers' Company, with the motto " Unto God only be honour and glory."

This re-edification, including the purchase of the land, cost the Drapers' Company upwards of £3000, from whose funds each of the poor people receive annually about six pounds.

ST. CHAD'S ALMSHOUSES

adjoin the cemetery of Old St. Chad's, and were erected in 1409 by Bennett Tipton, a public brewer, who lived in the College, and died in 1424. The allowance to the eleven poor occupants, " decayed old men and women," arises chiefly from a benefaction of £180 by David Ireland, alderman of the town, and Catharine his wife; which is now commuted to a rent charge of £8 on the Lythwood estate, the proprietor of which nominates the alms-folk. Previous to the Reformation the poor people received one penny a-week from the Mercers' Company, since which time the whole annual payment of the Company has been only two shillings and two pence.

HOUSE OF INDUSTRY.

This spacious and well-built structure stands on an eminence rising from the Severn, which forms a beautiful object beneath.   The site is highly salubrious, and the prospect delightfully variegated by many natural beauties. The majestic Wrekin, with an extensive tract of country, is seen to the right; while the front presents a very general view of the town, skirted by genteel residences partly obscured by the foliage of The Quarry trees, which, with the towers of the Castle, the lofty steeples of the churches and their glittering vanes, unite in producing a scene diversified and impressive, especially when the evening sun illumines the landscape, and gives to it that variety of light and shadow which poets have associated as only belonging to the scenes of enchantment and fairy land.

A fine terrace extends the whole length of the building, which was erected (in 1760) for the reception of orphans from the Foundling Hospital in London, at an expence of £12,000; but the funds of that institution not proving adequate to the plan of sending children to provincial hospitals, it was discontinued in 1774.   It afterwards served as a place of confinement for Dutch prisoners taken in the American war; and in 1784 it was purchased under an act of parliament for incorporating the five parishes of the town and that of Meole Brace in the liberties, so far as concerned the maintenance of the poor, as a general House of Industry for their admission and employment, under the management of a board of directors.

Various circumstances, however, have concurred to

render the establishment a complete failure, both as regards the principles on which it was founded, the economy to be effected, and the advantages eventually to result in favour of the united parishes, the select vestries of which now send but a small proportion of their poor, and those are generally infirm, who are maintained by a contractor, at a certain rate per head per week; but " averages " are still paid by the several parishes, to keep the extensive buildings in repair, for a salary to the chaplain, and other purposes of the institution, which continues under the ostensible government of directors.

The dining hall is 115 feet in length, parallel with which is a chapel of the same size, in which service is performed once every Sunday.

HUMANE SOCIETY.

A Humane Society existed in this town in the year 1786, but, having sunk from notice, was resuscitated in 1824, for the purpose of preventing those fatal accidents which have been of frequent occurrence during the bathing season, and often in the winter time, when the river in a frozen state affords the amusement of skaiting. The purpose of the society is to render prompt assistance in the use of the most approved means for restoring suspended animation, from whatever cause arising, and the rewarding of persons whose humane and intrepid exertions have been instrumental in saving life, or, although unsuccessful, such as to entitle their endeavours to the thanks of society.

To accomplish these objects, watchmen, prepared with every requisite apparatus, are stationed on the banks of the river, where accidents at any time may be expected to occur, and receiving houses are established, where every facility is afforded to employ remedies for the restoring of life in those cases which hold out the slightest hope of a recovery.

It may be mentioned that many instances have occurred by which a just estimate can be formed of the positive good resulting from the exertions of this Society, in rescuing persons from drowning.

THE PRISON CHARITIES

were commenced about the year 1800, for the distribution of rewards to promote the reformation and encourage the industry of criminals confined within the prison walls; to relieve the wants of unfortunate debtors; and to provide all those who are dismissed from prison with a small sum for immediate maintenance, so as to prevent the great temptation of committing crime for that purpose.

The annual subscription is limited to one guinea; and the institution has met with a laudable support, principally among the gentry of the county.

THE PAROCHIAL CHARITIES

of this town have at different times been largely endowed by the legacies of individuals who, in bidding the world adieu, were piously moved to leave portions of their substance to be expended in "bread to the poor," clothing and apprenticing poor children, annual gifts of money and garments to decayed housekeepers, and the general improvement of all, by directing commemorative sermons to be preached on particular anniversaries. In St. Chad's parish two hundred threepenny loaves are, on the average, distributed weekly throughout the year.

THE TOWN CHARITIES

were bequeathed for purposes in many respects similar to the foregoing, and were under the management of the old

Corporation; but by the provisions of the Municipal Act the distribution of them is vested in trustees appointed by the Lord Chancellor.

Several other charitable societies exist in the town, whose object is to afford gifts of money, clothing, medical assistance, and religious instruction, to the necessitous sick poor; as well as for the distribution of the scriptures and the public formularies of the established church, and for the propagation of christianity both at home and abroad, the detail of which would exceed the prescribed limits of this publication.

CHARITY SCHOOLS.

" TO LEARNING'S SECOND SEATS WE NOW PROCEED."

BOWDLER's, OR THE BLUE SCHOOL,

Is situated in Beeches Lane, and is an oblong brick building, having in the centre a glazed cupola, surmounted by a flying dragon. It was founded in 1724, according to the will of Mr. Thomas Bowdler, alderman and draper, for the instruction, clothing, and apprenticing poor children of the parish of St. Julian.

Eighteen boys and 12 girls receive their education here, and attend service at St. Julian's church on Sundays, to which church Mr. Bowdler was a great benefactor.— The number of scholars, from the increased value of the property belonging to the school, is about to be increased.

MILLINGTON's SCHOOL & HOSPITAL.

This excellent institution and monument of private munificence stands on an eminence in the suburb of Frankwell, which commands an extensive prospect of the town, its churches, public buildings, and more distant views.

The building consists of a handsome pedimented front, with a stone portico, and two wings attached to the centre by a row of houses; the summit is crowned by a bell turret.

The chapel occupies the centre of the building, and contains a portrait of the founder. Adjoining are residences for the master and mistress of the school, and twelve houses for the resident hospitallers.

The foundation was endowed by Mr. James Millington, a draper, of Shrewsbury, and consists (according to his will) of a school-master and mistress with liberal salaries, and a chaplain, whose duty it is to read prayers every school day at nine o'clock in the morning. The scholars, &c. attend St. George's church on Sundays.

Twelve poor men or women, chosen from the single parishioners living in Frankwell, or from the part of Saint Chad's parish nearest to it, have each a comfortable dwelling consisting of two apartments, and a good garden, with two gowns, or coats, three tons of coal and ten guineas yearly, and two loaves of bread weekly. Gowns and coats, with £4 per annum and two loaves weekly, are given to ten poor single housekeepers resident in Frankwell, the four senior of which occupy two chambers each above the school rooms, and are removed according to seniority into the hospital when a vacancy occurs.

The school rooms are in the rear of the building, in which twenty-five boys and as many girls receive their education, with clothing twice a-year. At the age of fourteen the boys are apprenticed, and £10 given as a premium with each; previous to which they are well clothed, and on producing a certificate of good behaviour during apprenticeship, £5 is presented as a gratuity. The girls are allowed £3 for clothing on leaving the school, and, on behaving well, at the expiration of three years of their service receive £3 more.

A Sermon is annually preached in St. Chad's church, on the 12th of August, according to the will of the founder, to commemorate his birth-day.

Two exhibitions of £40 a-year each are founded for students of St. Mary Magdalene College, Cambridge, eligible to those who have been originally scholars in the school and born in Frankwell, and educated at the Free Schools.

The charity is governed by fourteen trustees; and the revenues, by proper management, are considerable. Well may it be said, after reading this noble bequest—

" Behold what blessing wealth to life can lend."

ALLATT'S SCHOOL

Is situated in Murivance, near St. Chad's church, and was erected and endowed pursuant to the will of JOHN ALLATT, Gent. The building is an elegant free-stone structure, designed by Mr. Haycock in 1800, and cost £2000. It consists of two excellent houses for the master and mistress, which are connected with the schools by an arcade.

Thirty boys and thirty girls are educated and clothed, and at a proper age placed out as apprentices or servants.— Twenty-eight coats and 140 stuff gowns are annually given to poor men and women from the funds of the same charity.

The management of the school and funds is under the direction of fourteen trustees.

PUBLIC SUBSCRIPTION SCHOOL.

This school was begun by a subscription as early as the year 1708, for the instruction and clothing of poor children, and is conducted on the National system, in spacious school rooms near the east end of the English bridge. A sermon is preached annnally in aid of its funds

o

at two of the churches in the town. Nearly three hundred children receive daily education here, and on Sundays they attend the worship of the established church.

THE LANCASTERIAN SCHOOLS

were erected in 1812, opposite the County Gaol, for the plan of education suggested by the late Mr. Joseph Lancaster. They are supported by subscriptions and donations, with a small weekly contribution from the scholars.

ST. MARY'S AND ST. MICHAEL'S SCHOOLS

are situated in the suburb of Castle Foregate, and were erected in 1832, in the old English style of architecture, from a design by Mr. John Carline. Two hundred and fifty boys and girls receive their daily instruction, and are taken to St. Michael's church twice on Sundays.

The school is supported by private benefactions; and the National system of education is adopted.

ST. CHAD'S LADIES' SCHOOL

is held in the remains of Old St. Chad's church, and the mode of tuition practised is that of the Madras system, which has been in operation in this school since 1820.

The number of girls educated is 154, under the care of visitors, whose aim, as expressed in the report of the school, is " to be instrumental in bringing up poor children in the fear of God, and in instilling into them such religious principles as may lead them to do their duty, for conscience sake, in that state of life to which it shall please God to call them." The girls are clothed annually, and the total expence of the school is rather more than £100 a year, nearly one-half of which is contributed by the children in the shape of earnings and a penny fund, the remainder by subscriptions and donations.

INFANT SCHOOLS

produce a wide field for useful exertion, by forming the disposition and giving an early moral bias to the mind;—if, indeed, they do no more than take young children from the debasing influence under which their characters must otherwise be formed, and present an example of a better kind, they are calculated to effect a good purpose.

Schools having this object in view are established in the suburbs of FRANKWELL, CASTLE FOREGATE, and COLEHAM, and are supported by subscriptions under the direction of intelligent ladies.

SUNDAY SCHOOLS.

There are several Sunday Schools connected with the established church and the different congregations of dissenters, some of which have existed nearly from the earliest formation of such institutions.

A WALK WITHIN THE WALLS.

HAVING noticed the principal Public Structures and Charitable Institutions of Shrewsbury, we turn next to those objects and ancient remains which do not admit of a regular classification.

In adapting the present work, therefore, to assist the Stranger, it is proposed to notice these and such other localities that may engage and deserve attention, in the course of A WALK WITHIN THE WALLS of our town, replete in subjects of antiquarian interest.

In the survey of these matters we shall occasionally lose sight of the refinement of modern times, and accommodate our thoughts and feelings to the days of yore, by adding such historical remarks as may serve the purpose of general as well as local information.

Our perambulation will commence from the spacious area in front of the County Hall, called the

MARKET SQUARE,

from the vegetable market being held there, and from whence may be seen several good specimens of the half-timbered houses of our forefathers, terminating with lofty gables.

Proceeding up HIGH STREET, anciently called " Bakers' Row," from the number of that occupation which located there : on the left of the turning towards Grope Lane is an old timbered house, now a grocer's shop, but formerly used as

THE MERCERS' HALL.

Several of the Incorporated Companies originally possessed Halls for holding their meetings and the celebration of their feasts : the former have of late years been held at the Town Hall, and the latter at some of the inns.

About the middle of the street, on the right, is the Unitarian Meeting House (p. 95), where the poet Coleridge preached in 1798 ;* and a few yards further is the " Sextry" passage, or (as it is called in our provincialism) a " shut." This originally communicated with St. Chad's church-yard by a covered passage, and derived its name from the sacristy of the church, which is supposed to have stood within it. An old building, now the " Golden Cross," appears to have been a tavern as early as the year 1495, for in the archives of the corporation is the charge of 13s. 2d. " for wine spent on the king's gentlemen in the Sextrie." Its gloomy and confined situation proves how little our unpolished ancestors regarded accommodation or prospect when they were enjoying the pleasure of a jovial carouse.

The ancient stone building at the extremity of the street was in times past occupied as the

SHEARMEN'S HALL ;

since which it has been used as a theatre, a methodist chapel, an assembly room, and a temporary assize court ; and although now modernised as a tea warehouse, the present remains convey much of the character of the " city halls"

o 3

* Vide Hazlitt's Literary Remains.

of other days, associated with the good cheer, inspirating feasts, and the social merriment of com-brethren in the olden time.

The period of its erection is not known; but before the front was altered it presented (according to a drawing in the possession of the writer) a bold pointed window in the style of the fifteenth century, the apex of the gable being finished with an elegant finial. On the south-west side a very curious octagonal chimney, crenelated at the top, still remains.

The company of Shearmen were incorporated at least as early as the reign of Edward the Fourth, and the extracts preserved from their records afford many pleasing particulars of ancient customs and hospitality. The setting up of a " green tree," or May-pole, before their hall, " deck'd with garlands gay," was, according to an old MS. an usage practised by the apprentices of this company on their feast-day (June 6th) previous to the year 1588. The noisy revelry connected therewith, and of

" Lads and lasses dancing round,"

seems to have excited the displeasure of the puritans, and the custom having been denounced by the " public preacher of the town,"* and forbidden by the bailiffs, the MS. further says, that " in 1591 certain young men for their disobedience were put into prison and indicted at the sessions, but on their submission they were acquit of their disobedience, and all further proceedings against them quashed, and it was determined that the usual tree might be put up as heretofore, so that it be done soberly and in good order, without contention." The attempt to obstruct this ancient festivity caused an angry cavilling and interchange of written communications between the favourers of it and the bailiffs, so as to raise an opposition at the annual passing of the town accounts, for the expence incurred by the prosecution.

In the reign of Elizabeth, six hundred shearmen or cloth-workers were occupied (under the drapers) in dressing or raising the wool on one side of a coarse kind of cloth called Welsh webs, which were brought from Merionethshire and Montgomeryshire to a weekly market in this town.

This manner of raising the wool having been found to

* An office instituted when preaching was not frequent, and granted to the Minister of St. Mary's in the reign of Queen Elizabeth.

weaken the texture of the cloths, the avocation of the company became useless and was discontinued.

Leaving St. Julian's Church (p. 59) on the left, we arrive at the WYLE COP,—cop is the Saxon word for top, or head of any thing, and this part is considered as the first portion of the town inhabited by the early British settlers, being situated near the royal dwelling of Brochwel (the site of Old St. Chad's church). The Saxons, on their possession of the town, continued (without doubt) for a time to occupy the huts abandoned by the Britons. From hence the town extended itself northward in the direction of the churches. Proceeding down the Wyle Cop, we pass the LION HOTEL ; four doors below is the house which formed the temporary residence of King Henry the Seventh, who, although he left the bailiffs to pay his soldiers, did not forget the favour conferred upon him by the burgesses. From this place is a pretty distant view of the Wrekin, Lord Hill's Column, &c. At the foot of the Wyle, and turning to the right, we leave on the left the precinct of the GREY FRIARS, and pass along *Beeches Lane*, anciently *Bispestan* and *Bushpestanes*, in which is the Blue School and the Roman Catholic Chapel, and arrive at

THE TOWN WALLS,

erected in the time of Henry the Third, to fortify the place against the inroads of the Welsh, and towards the completion of which the burgesses were materially assisted by the royal bounty. These walls, although now deprived of their battlements, form an excellent footpath, and afford a delightful view of the river and adjacent country. At the extremity of the Walls is the *Crescent ;* and a little beyond stands the only remaining Tower of nearly twenty which formerly strengthened the ancient ramparts that enclosed our town.

It is square, and of three stories, embattled at the summit, and lighted by narrow square windows; from the style
of building, it is probably as old as the reign of Henry the
Fourth.

Nearly adjoining the Tower is the Meeting-house of
the Methodist New Connexion; and further on to the right
is *Swan Hill*, formerly called *Murivance*, signifying before
or within the walls. Passing Allatt's School, a chaste free-
stone building, the turning to the right leads to *St. John's
Hill*, chiefly occupied by private individuals. Proceeding
onwards, St. Chad's church breaks upon the view, having a
terrace on the south-west side which commands a fine
prospect of the beautiful QUARRY WALK. Leaving the
principal entrance to this delightful promenade, a broad
thoroughfare leads to the handsome residences of *Claremont Buildings*. Continuing our route to the end of this
street, a narrow way opens to St. Austin's Friars and the

river, on the margin of which once stood an out-work, flanked by two round towers, erected by the corporation at a remote period for the protection of the opposite ford. In later times one of these towers was called the " Round House," and was demolished about forty years ago. Turning to the right, we observe the remnant of the house of

THE AUSTIN FRIARS,

of which little appears excepting the outer portion of a red stone building, now used as a tan-house. The Friars Eremites of St. Augustine are supposed to have located in this town about the middle of the thirteenth century, and erected their house on a site which had been used during the reign of John as a place of sepulture, interment in consecrated ground having for a period been forbidden by that king.

The following beautiful initial letter, affixed to a

charter from Edward the Third, in 1345, assigns to the friars of this convent the out-work above alluded to, under certain conditions, with leave to have a postern gate for ingress and egress towards their house and church.

The king is depicted as sitting upon his throne, holding a globe in his left and a sceptre in his right hand, with two friars kneeling before him, and a third presenting a book or charter.

In the church of this Priory was a sanctuary, where a murderer could take refuge, and thereby escape his merited punishment; and several knights and men of rank, slain in the battle of Shrewsbury, were buried within its walls.

Previously to the dissolution, this house, like many others, fell suddenly into a state of bankruptcy, and the church was stripped of its furniture and vestments. On the site of the precinct which once pertained to this friary, and extended to the Quarry walk, several good houses have been erected.

On the opposite side of the river is the suburb of Frankwell, bordered with gardens; Millington's Hospital crowning the eminence.

THE WELSH BRIDGE

next attracts attention. It is a bold and substantial structure, completed in 1795, from a design by Messrs. Tilley and Carline, of this town, at a cost of £8000. It consists of five semi-circular arches, surmounted with a balustrade, and is 266 feet in length and 30 in breadth.

It has been truly remarked, that while in cities of greater commercial importance no public works of great extent have been carried on without the exaction of tolls and contributions, the inhabitants of this town and county have, to their immortal honour, erected two noble bridges, by which the trade of the neighbouring districts has been released from the burthen of a vexatious tax, at a total expence of full £30,000, the whole of which was raised by voluntary contribution.

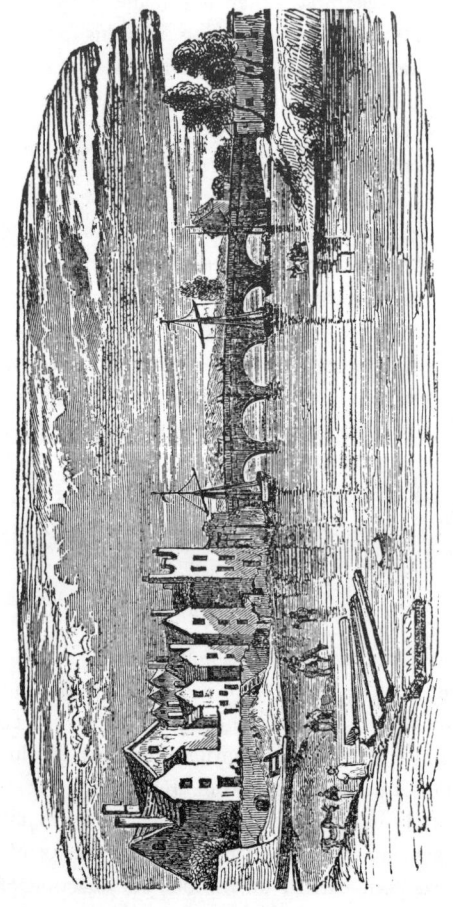

THE WELSH BRIDGE.

It is, however, matter of regret that too little attention has been shewn to encroachments on the river, by which much of the beauty of our bridges has been destroyed.

Adjoining the Welsh bridge are quays and spacious warehouses, from whence the barges and trows receive and discharge their cargoes. This end of the town formerly displayed a scene of commercial importance, as being the place where the London, Birmingham, and Manchester waggons arrived, and from whence goods were forwarded to all parts of the kingdom; but owing to the communication opened with the above-mentioned places by the Shrewsbury canal, which terminates in the Castle-foregate, most of the goods arrive there; this part, therefore, retains little more of its former bustle than is occasioned by the arrival of waggons for the dispatch of merchandize into North Wales, and what remains of the Severn trade.

From hence we proceed up the street called MARDOL; about half-way up, on the right, is HILL'S LANE, where is situated

ROWLEY'S MANSION,

said to be the first brick structure erected in Shrewsbury. It appears to have been built in 1618 by William Rowley, draper, and the first of his family who settled in this town, of which he was admitted a burgess in 1594, and made an alderman in 1633, under the charter of Charles the First. His grand-daughter and co-heiress married John Hill, Esq. who lived in great hospitality in this mansion, from whom the street received the appellation of *Hill's Lane*, instead of Knuckin-street. He died in 1731, and the house was soon afterwards inhabited by the talented Dr. Adams, incumbent of St. Chad's from 1731 to 1775.

The portal of this mansion is curious, and is accurately delineated by the wood cut. The great chamber, or withdrawing room, remains nearly in its original state, and is adorned with a basso relievo representation of the Creation,

and other devices in stucco, &c.   The oak wainscot from
the other apartments has lately been removed.   It is now

used as a storehouse for grain, and presents a striking picture of—

> " Some banquet Hall deserted,
> Whose lights are fled, whose glory's dead,
> And all but it departed."

Retracing our steps to Mardol, at the top of the street
is a pile of ancient houses, decorated on the exterior with

plaster and stone ornaments, in the fantastical fashion of
the time in which they were built. The turning below
these leads to *Claremont Street*, formerly Doglane. On
the left is a curious half-timbered house, built in 1613, with
a projecting porch. A little lower is the Baptist Meeting
House. Keeping to the left, is an old mansion, called

THE BELL STONE,

from a large stone which formerly stood outside the wall
that surrounded the portion of the court not occupied by
the buildings. The stone is now removed to the area in
front of the house, which before the recent alteration was a
good specimen of the smaller mansion of the reign of Queen
Elizabeth. It was erected by Edward Owen, Esq. a bailiff
of the town in 1582.

Leaving the new Theatre on the right, we enter the
street called SHOPLATCH, a name supposed to be derived
from SHUTT PLACE, the residence of an ancient Shrewsbury
family of the name of Shutt, the remains of which are still
to be traced in the massive walls of a stone edifice long
disused, however, for domestic purposes, and arrive at
Mardol Head, formerly called THE STALLS. At the corner
leading to High-street is

IRELAND'S MANSION,

once the town residence of the ancient family of Ireland,
long seated at Albrighton. It is a spacious half-timbered
building, four stories high, finished with gables, on the
beams of which are the following armorial bearings—Gules,
three fleurs de lis, three, two, and one, Argent. The front
consists of four ranges of bay windows, the original entrance
having been in the centre under a Tudor arch. It is now
divided into three excellent dwellings.

Passing up PRIDE HILL, formerly called Corvisors' Row, we reach the High Pavement, where, opposite the present Butter and Poultry Market, once stood

THE HIGH CROSS,

which was no doubt similar in design to the elegant structures at Chichester and other places.   It appears to have escaped the iconoclastic zeal of the puritans; for we learn that the old stone cross was not taken down until the year 1705.   All general proclamations, as in former times, are still made upon this spot, whilst the reminiscences connected with it afford a melancholy picture of feudal severity. Here David, the last of the British Princes, underwent his cruel sentence, for defending by force of arms the liberties of his native country; and here the Earl of Worcester and other distinguished noblemen, after the battle of Shrewsbury, atoned for their rebellion by the loss of their heads.

Continuing our course, we enter CASTLE STREET, which is terminated in a picturesque manner by Laura's tower on the Castle mount, and the umbrageous foliage with which it is surrounded.   At the extremity of this spacious street stands

ST. NICHOLAS'S CHAPEL,

the only one existing of eight similar structures. Its present appearance proves it to be of Norman foundation, and built probably by Earl Roger de Montgomery for the accommodation of such of his retainers as resided in the *outer court* of the castle within which it once stood.   It was subsequently appropriated for the accommodation of the President and Council of the Marches of Wales.   The west end displays a pointed window divided by a mullion, and in the interior is a massive semi-circular arch, which separated the nave from a chancel now destroyed.   In lowering the floor

in 1825, several human skulls and bones were discovered.
The building is 50 feet long, by 19 wide, and is used at
present as a coach-house and stable.

To the right of this edifice is a handsome timber gateway, erected in 1620, which leads to

THE COUNCIL HOUSE,

or LORD'S PLACE, originally occupied as the residence of

P 3

the Court of the Marches of Wales; the Lords President and Council of which, in assembling,

> " With temper'd awe to guide
> An old and haughty nation proud in arms,"

were frequently received here " righte royallie" by the corporation and trading companies; the latter, no doubt, considering that the great number of persons which this Court attracted to the town in its judicial capacity, independent of the attendant pomp and feasting, was of no small benefit to them in their respective crafts and occupations, by multiplying the consumption of the necessaries of life, and imparting to Shrewsbury somewhat of the importance of a second capital.

In the early part of the rebellion, the Corporation sent an invitation to Charles the First, stating that he should " have free access into the town, and be entertained in the best manner these troublesome times afford." The unfortunate monarch accepted the loyal offer of his Salopian subjects, and arrived here Sept. 20th, 1642, attended by his two sons (the Prince of Wales and the Duke of York) and his nephew Prince Rupert, where he resided for the space of six weeks. King James the Second also kept his court here in 1687.

In 1583 the Corporation granted to Richard Barker, Esq. town-clerk of Shrewsbury, their interest in the council house and adjoining chapel, reserving the use of it for the annual residence of her Majesty's Council. From him it passed to Thomas Owen, Esq. also town-clerk, in whose family it remained until it was purchased by Richard Lyster, Esq. to whose descendant, Henry Lyster, of Rowton Castle, Esq. it now belongs.*

* On the visit of Charles the First to this venerable mansion, Thomas Lyster (among other distinguished Shropshire loyalists) presented that Prince

The building stands on an eminence overhanging the
river in the vicinity of the castle, in what is supposed to
have been the outer ballium of that fortress.   Its erection
took place about the time of Henry the Seventh, and it was
soon afterwards considerably enlarged in all probability with
some of the materials from the castle and the adjoining
convent of Black Friars.   On the extinction of the Court
of the Marches in 1689, these extensive buildings became
ruinous, and their remains have been (during the present
century) converted into three good houses, which command delightful prospects.   The hall and great chamber
above form a portion of the residence of Dr. Du Gard, who
has displayed a commendable taste in preserving as far as
possible the character of this part of the building.

Returning along Castle Street, on the right is the
Raven Hotel, where Lieut. Geo. Farquhar (in 1704 or
1705) wrote his comedy of " The Recruiting Officer," the
scene of which is laid in Shrewsbury; and while it sufficiently demonstrates he was well acquainted with that gay
scene of life which forms the subject of his play, it is
equally certain he had " living originals in his eye."   The
epistle dedicatory is " To all friends round the Wrekin,"
and states he was a perfect stranger to every thing in Salop
but its character of loyalty, the number of its inhabitants,
and their generous and hospitable reception of strangers,—
an eulogium, it is devoutly to be wished, may be retained
by Salopians in every generation.

Taking the direction of the street opposite the Raven,
a pleasing view of ancient and modern architecture presents

with a purse of £500.   His grandson, Richard Lyster, Esq. represented this
town and county in parliament for a period of forty-five years, and was known
among his countrymen by the familiar appellation of ' THE SENATOR.'   The
somewhat feudal cast of his establishment, and most ample scale of ancient
English hospitality, are pleasingly recorded in the " Sheriffs of Shropshire."

itself, in St. Mary's church and the Infirmary.   On the
south-west side of the church-yard is

THE DRAPERS' HALL,

a half-timbered building, erected probably about the time of
Elizabeth.   The interior is sufficiently described by the
accompanying engraving, presented by the liberality of the

Drapers' Company. The apartment is 28 feet by 20, but was originally of larger dimensions. It is wainscotted with fine old oak, and the floor was once rich in emblazoned tiles. At the north end is the upper place, or " dais." where the members " feasted full and high;" and on the opposite side stands a fine old chest, with richly carved ornaments; above which is a painting said to represent the first steward of the company, Degory Watur, and his wife; this originally stood on the front of the hall house occupied by Degory in the almshouses.

The east side is decorated with a portrait of Edward the Fourth, denoting round the circumference his titles and decease in 1483. Beneath are the following lines:—

> This Yeare fourth Edward York's farre fam'd renowne
> Circled his temples with great Albion's crowne;
> When over reading the memoriale
> Of Salop's Draper's Ancient Hospitale,
> Founded in honour of the sacred Deity,
> He own'd and stiled them then, the blest Society;
> And with his Parliament's sage approbation
> Deigned them his Charter for a Corporation,
> Which to confirme Himself was pleas'd to be
> The Royal Founder of their Companie,
> Granting immunities of large extent,
> Which stand his bounties gratefull monument.

> Edwardo 4° regi Anglorum
> Gloriosissimo monumentum
> Hoc posuit Pannariorum
> Salopiensium grata Societas.

Returning from this hall, which is the only one appropriated to its original purpose, to the left is DOGPOLE (from Doke or Duck, to decline, and Poll, the head or summit); the street having an abrupt descent towards the river, to which there was formerly a communication.

To the right is St. Mary's Street and the Almshouses, This street was very narrow until the year 1824, when several old buildings were taken down.   Pursuing our course along CHURCH STREET, we pass the site and remnant of a half-timbered house, distinguished by gables, which formed a portion of

JONES'S MANSION,

in which the Duke of York resided when he accompanied his royal father to this town in 1642.   It was also the abode of " Prince Rupert, when he joined his uncle after the brilliant action of Worcester."   This house was built by Thos. Jones, Esq. whose burial is noticed in the account of the adjoining church of St. Alkmond.   Leaving that sacred edifice to the left, and turning a few yards to the right, we arrive at the DOUBLE BUTCHER ROW, a street chiefly occupied by butcher's shambles, and where is an

ANCIENT TIMBER HOUSE,

considered to be one of the oldest and largest of this kind of buildings of which our town displays so many specimens.

The projecting stories are sustained by elegant brackets, and the angle uprights enriched with small pointed arches, carved with trefoil and other decorations.   Along the front basement is a cloister of wooden arches obtusely pointed.— This building, 60 feet in length, is now divided into smaller habitations.   History is silent as to the time, or by whom this edifice was erected, nor have we any decided information of its primary occupancy.

From the appearance of the cloister, it has been conjectured that it was a religious house, inhabited by the chauntry priets of the fraternity of the Holy Cross in St. Alkmund's church.   But from its extent it is more likely to have been the town mansion of the Abbot of Lilleshull, who had a residence in this part of the parish, and to which monastery the patronage of the church belonged.

Continuing our route to the left of this house, we pass steps leading to the churchyard, and the foundations of a stone building (which once pertained to an *Oriel* and the ancient college of St. Alkmond), into Fish-street, occupied by shambles, and on market-days by the country butchers. Crossing the top of High-street, we enter Milk-street, which leads to Old St. Chad's (page 28), and the street called BELMONT, in which is situated

THE JUDGES' HOUSE,

purchased by the County of Salop in 1821, under an act for
providing suitable accommodation for the reception of his
Majesty's judges of assize.   At the south-west end of the
opposite thoroughfare across the church-yard is the remains
of a red stone wall which formed part of

THE COLLEGE OF ST. CHAD,

originally a large ancient building inclosing a quadrangular
court, separated from the street by a lofty wall and gateway.
In 1549 Edward the Sixth granted the college to Hugh
Edwards, Esq. the individual who (in 1551) exerted himself
in obtaining the foundation of our grammar school.   It
continued in his family until 1752, when Lord and Lady
Malpas disposed of the buildings, which were soon afterwards
converted into three excellent houses, but so effectually
modernized with brick as to display none of the appearance
of a " college," although the name is still retained.

Westward is College Hill.   Half-way down this street,
a modern Gothic front denotes

VAUGHAN'S PLACE,

which, before its alteration and brick casing in 1795, was
considered a most curious specimen of the unembattled
town mansion, erected (it is conjectured) about the middle
of the fourteenth century by Sir Hamo Vaughan, whose
daughter Eleanor married Reginald de Mutton.   By this
alliance the house came into the possession of the Myttons
of Halston, several of whom represented this town in parliament; but little of its original state now appears.   The
hall is approached from a passage near the Corn-market by
a flight of steps, and displays a deeply-recessed pointed
arch; a similar one is seen from the College-hill entrance.
One portion of the building forms the WATCH ROOM and

POLICE STATION of the town, and some of the spacious vaults beneath are used as a temporary receptacle for midnight disorderlies.

Nearly adjoining, in the street leading to the Cornmarket, is the TALBOT HOTEL, where the Duchess of Kent and the Princess Victoria alighted on their visit to this town in 1832, on which occasion the mayor and corporation waited upon them with a congratulatory address.

———••◦◉◉◦◉◦◉◉◦••———

LITERARY AND SCIENTIFIC INSTITUTIONS.

SHROPSHIRE AND NORTH WALES NATURAL HISTORY AND ANTIQUARIAN SOCIETY.

At a meeting held at Shrewsbury on the 26th of June, 1835, it was resolved to establish a Natural History Society for the county of Salop and North Wales, and to found a central museum and scientific library.

In order to secure the perpetuity of the institution, and to guard against the possible dispersion of the museum at any future period, the property of the society is vested in the lords lieutenant of the county of Salop, and of the several counties of North Wales, as trustees, for the permanent use and benefit of the district at large.

The museum is principally designed to illustrate the Natural History of the district, in its various branches of geology, mineralogy, zoology, and botany, by the gradual formation of complete and systematic arrangements of its productions, in each of these departments.   It is also open

Q

to other objects of scientific interest, and in particular is a suitable repository for such remains of antiquity as are found within the district, or illustrate its general history. But, in addition to these more local objects, the museum will, it is anticipated, through the liberality of the friends of science in various quarters, be enriched with many specimens from distant places.

The library consists of Books illustrative of Natural History and Antiquities, and such works of reference as the funds of the society may admit of being purchased, for the illustration of the objects in the museum. The library, as well as the museum, is open to donations from the members and friends of the institution.

The society's affairs are under the management of a council, consisting of a president and other officers, elected annually.

A house situated in Dogpole is at present the temporary repository for the collections of the Museum, &c.

THE SUBSCRIPTION LIBRARY

Is on St. John's Hill, and contains an excellent collection of books in the various departments of literature and science. Its affairs are confided to a committee. Proprietary members pay two guineas admission, and an annual subscription of one guinea and a half; and strangers, on the introduction of a subscriber, have the privilege of consulting any of the books during library hours.

THE NEW CHORAL SOCIETY

Has for its design the cultivation of the delightful science of sacred music, and was revived in 1834. It is under the management of a secretary and committee, and is supported by a respectable number of honorary members.

THE HORTICULTURAL SOCIETY

was engrafted (in the year 1834) on a florists' society planted in this town in 1823. Its object is to promote the culture of the auricula, polyanthus, pink, ranunculus, carnation, picotee, dahlia, gooseberry, &c.

MECHANICS' INSTITUTION.

This institution commenced in 1825, and in the year 1833 a building was erected for their meetings in Howard-street, Castle-foregate. The expences of the establishment are defrayed by subscriptions and donations.

NEWSPAPERS.

Two weekly newspapers are published here: viz. *Wednesday*, THE SALOPIAN JOURNAL, by Mr. John Eddowes, Corn-market. *Friday*, THE SHREWSBURY CHRONICLE, by Mr. John Watton, St. John's-hill.

WALK WITHOUT THE WALLS.

"Scenes must be beautiful which daily view'd
Please daily, and whose novelty survives
Long knowledge and the scrutiny of years.
Praise justly due to those I now describe."

SHREWSBURY QUARRY.

On the south-western side of the town is one of the most celebrated promenades in the kingdom, called The Quarry.

It is formed in a tract of verdant meadow ground of twenty-three acres, gradually sloping to the river Severn, along the banks of which are planted a graceful avenue of lime trees, extending 540 yards in length, whose lofty arching branches entwine themselves so as to resemble the long aisle of some religious fane.

Three other walks, planted in a similar manner, serve as approaches from the town to this the principal promenade, which being enlivened with many pleasing views, renders it in point of situation and beauty unrivalled.

Here the inhabitant may inhale the refreshing breeze wafted from the rippling river,—the invalid find a cool and sequestered retreat free from the noise of a bustling town,—while the mind alive to the charms of nature may enjoy its philosophic contemplations in the ever-changing beauties of the seasons.

A cluster of horse-chesnut and other trees growing in a dingle, and which in autumn present a beautifully variegated mass of foliage, diversify what otherwise might be considered a formal arrangement of these walks, which were planted during the mayoralty of Henry Jenks, Esq. in 1719, and derive their name from a red sandstone which was formerly procured from this dingle.

On the opposite side of the meandering river is a verdant eminence fringed with luxuriant plantations.

At the north-western end of the Quarry, near Claremont, is a sloping bank, which originally formed an amphitheatre, called the " Dry Dingle," where religious mysteries (or miracle plays) were celebrated. Prince Arthur, in 1494, attended one of these exhibitions, which were performed on this spot, even after the Reformation, by the head-schoolmaster, Mr. Ashton, and his pupils.

Crossing the ferry, at the extremity of the walk leading from the remains of this amphitheatre, and pursuing the footpath in the field to the left of the Boat-house, we reach an eminence from whence a prospect opens to the view combining water, hill, plain, and wood in charming variety. Continuing from hence to the right of the House of Industry, we arrive at

KINGSLAND,

or, as written in an early Norman grant, *Chingsland*. This is an extensive piece of land, belonging to the ancient burgesses of Shrewsbury, thirty of whom in rotation annually receive four shillings and sixpence from its produce, in lieu of a " turn for their kine." On this place the festival of Shrewsbury Show (described page 109) is held, and it commands a prospect which stretches to a considerable distance over a beautiful and well-cultivated country, diversified with mountains possessing form and interest.

Returning to the front of the House of Industry, and

pursuing the path from the bank on which that building stands, we cross the Severn by means of the ferry at the Can Office, and enter the pastures called " *Stury's Close*," where the Earl of Pembroke, Lord President of the Marches, " mustered all the country, both of horsemen and footmen," in 1588 (a year memorable for the defeat of the Invincible Armada), and soon reach

THE GREY OR FRANCISCAN FRIARY.

The remnant illustrated by the wood cut comprises probably the refectory, which was partly re-edificed as late as the reign of Henry the Eighth.

This religious society, sometimes called Friars Minors, settled in this town early in the thirteenth century. Hawis, wife to Charleton Lord of Powys (born in 1291), and heir of the ancient Princes of Powys Gwenwynwyn, was a great benefactress to this friary, if not its second foundress.

From the quantity of bones which have been found within the precinct of this convent, it would seem that no unprofitable use was made of the privilege granted to this order by the Pope of "*liberam sepulturam.*" This and their reputed sanctity, as well as the popular belief that whoever was buried in their cemetery or in the habit of a grey friar would be secure from the attacks of evil spirits and find an easy entrance into heaven, were circumstances doubtless of such importance as to induce many persons to desire sepulture among such hallowed men.

The splendid stained glass now in the eastern window of St. Mary's chancel is supposed to have originally decorated the church of this friary, which was the burial place of the Lords of Powys.

On the opposite side of the river is the foundry and the suburb of Coleham.

Passing under the arch of the English Bridge, to the left are some modern dwellings on the site of a curious half-timbered mansion erected in the reign of Elizabeth by William Jones, an alderman and opulent draper of the town, and father of Thomas Jones, the first mayor of Shrewsbury. A view and description of this curious building, communicated by the author of these pages, will be found in vol. 99, part ii. of the Gentleman's Magazine.

A few yards beyond stood

THE DOMINICAN FRIARY,

which comprehended nearly the whole space now occupied by gardens between the bridge and the water gate.*

This order of mendicants took their name from their founder, and were sometimes called " Preachers" from their office, and " Black Friars" from their dress.

The convent, like those of the Austin and Franciscan friars, was placed on the margin of the river, outside the walls and adjacent to the bridges.

From the rich architectural remains, &c. which have occasionally been dug up here, the church must have been a spacious and elegant building; but, in common with the other convents, it shared the fate of the dissolution of monasteries, and was sold by Henry the Eighth in 1543. The hand of man, combined with the operations of time, had, previously to 1823, left but few vestiges either of the convent where Richard and George Plantagenet, two sons of Edward the Fourth, were born, or the more recent fortifications erected on this interesting spot,—where several military transactions were determined in various periods of our domestic history.

The bank on which this friary stood was levelled in the above-mentioned year, when the foundations of several walls were cleared to a considerable extent, and numerous capitals, pieces of mullions, with remains of stained glass, enamelled tiles, &c. were discovered by the workmen employed in the construction of a new building and wharf. Several stone graves were also brought to view, the masonry of which was well finished, and formed so as nearly to fit the corpse. After clearing the soil from these tombs, skele-

* The sloping bank above this friary was given to and occupied by the Monks of Shrewsbury Abbey, as a VINEYARD, as early as the reign of Henry the Third. Its situation on the northern side of the river, inclining southward and open to the east, renders it well adapted to the purpose.

tons were found encased in red sand, but without the least trace of any thing in which the body might have been enveloped. The only remains of this once noble pile are the materials used in the construction of a stable and the wall surrounding the gardens. Adjoining is

THE WATER-LANE GATE,

Through which the parliamentary army entered, Feb. 22d, 1644-5, and captured the town. The means by which this was accomplished showed much generalship and secrecy on

the part of the Parliamentarians. It appears a detachment of soldiers belonging to that party left Wem, and marched under the shadow of night to the extremity of the Castle-foregate, where the troopers halted at four o'clock in the morning, in order that the foot soldiers might effect an entrance by stratagem. The infantry turned off on the left to the river, being led by a puritanical minister of the town, named Huson, a kinsman of the celebrated John Huson, who from a cobbler rose to be a colonel and a member of the Barebones parliament.

The dismounted troopers were under the command of Benbow, who, being a native of Shrewsbury, was aware of the part most easily attacked. From the end of Castle-foregate they advanced through the fields to the castle ditch (now a thoroughfare), which was defended on the town side by strong palisading and a breastwork of earth. A boat on the river contained several carpenters and other persons, who commenced sawing down the paling near the river to effect a passage for the soldiers. This was soon accomplished, and by assisting one another over the ditch the breastwork was gained. Having succeeded thus far, they seem to have divided themselves into two divisions; the one party, headed by Benbow, scaled the wall on the eminence between the Watch Tower and the Council House, by means of light ladders. The main body, consisting of 350 men, entered by the gate shewn in the engraving, to which a tower and outwork was formerly attached. This, and a similar fort about the middle of the lane where the town wall crossed, yielded without resistance by the connivance of careless and treacherous sentinels, who are supposed to have been intoxicated and privy to the design. The party who had scaled the wall hastened to procure an entrance at the north or castle gate, which was soon done, and having let down the draw-bridge, the horse, with

Colonels Mytton and Bowyer at their head, made the best of their way to the main court of guard held in the Market-place, where they found their comrades engaged with the royalists. The loss on both sides was inconsiderable, amounting to only seven men and one captain. The castle surrendered about noon, when the garrison was immediately marched off to Ludlow, with the exception of thirteen poor Irishmen, who, being left to the tender mercies of the parliamentary leaders, were hanged the same day without trial.

Continuing the walk by the side of the river, the most prominent object is the tower on the castle mount, from whose lofty height a group of majestic trees decline to the banks of the Severn, which in this part bends gracefully over its gravelly bed. The pathway brings us to the island where a pageant took place in honour of Sir Philip Sidney (noticed page 11). A little beyond, on the opposite side of the river, is the ferry for conveying horses across by which barges are towed up the stream.* The meadows into which we have passed comprised a portion of the ancient Derfald, or enclosure for the keeping of deer,—in other words a park, which may not inaptly be called

SHREWSBURY PARK,

for it belonged to our first Norman earl, and in all probability to some of the Saxon monarchs. The situation of the ground, before it was stripped of its timber, possessed every advantage of pasture, water, and diversified surface.— According to the record of Domesday, it was the custom, when the king resided here, for twelve of the better sort of citizens to keep watch over him; and when he went out hunting, those having horses protected him. This practice

* This ferry leads to a walk which commands a bold view of the town, and communicates with the Abbey-foregate. It conducts also to the Under-dale Tea Gardens—a quiet rural retreat.

probably arose in consequence of the murder of Alfhelm (an earl of the blood royal) in 1016, who, having been invited here and hospitably entertained by Ædric Streona (son-in-law to King Etheldred), was barbarously assassinated by a butcher while hunting, whom the perfidious Ædric had engaged for that purpose.

The boundaries of these pleasant fields bring us to the Shrewsbury canal, which for some distance beyond passes above the banks of the river; while from the canal towing-path numerous pleasing views may be obtained, affording an agreeable half-hour's walk to the picturesque village of Uffington.

Retracing our steps along the green banks of the Severn, we arrive at a gentle ascent which leads to the promenade surrounding the prison. From hence the long ridge of Haughmond Hill, linked as it were to the noble Wrekin,—the stately character of the White Hall,—the patriotic Column in honour of Lord Hill,—the venerable Abbey Church, standing like a patriarch among its more modern compeers,—the Stretton Hills in the distance, and close at hand the frowning walls of the Castle, clad by nature's hand with stains of sober hue, combine to attract the eye and the mind.

On a line with the front of the County Prison is

HOWARD-STREET,

having at the top a fine colossal figure of Hercules, which was cast at Rome from the Farnese Hercules, and is no inapt memorial of the labour consequent upon the removal of upwards of 26,000 loads of soil in the formation of the street.

Passing to the DANA WALK, " where the huge castle hold its state," the prospect is bounded to the right by the eminences of Hawkstone, Grinshill, Pimhill, Almond Park, and the plain of " Battlefield." Westward is Berwick House, embosomed in sylvan beauty, and beyond in the horizon are a range of Cambrian mountains, gradually fading into the clouds, which in point of colour they not unfrequently resemble. Among these may be particularly distinguished those gigantic landmarks between England and Wales,—the Breidden and Moelygolfa hills. The former rises to the height of 1000 feet, and has on the summit a pillar erected to commemorate the great victory obtained by Admiral Rodney over the French fleet in the West Indies, 1782.

By a modern archway opened through the wall abutting from the Castle at the time this walk was formed, in 1790, we are again brought within the walls. This part, however, of

THE TOWN WALLS

extended in a line with the Castle Gates across the isthmus down to the banks of the river, having a corresponding barrier on the other side of the castle. It was erected by Robert de Belesme, third Norman Earl of Shrewsbury, under the idea that his father's fortifications were not of sufficient strength to withstand a siege from the forces of Henry I. which in 1102 marched against him (page 14).

An additional rampart called Roushill, enclosing the space between the wall of Earl Robert and the Welsh bridge, was added during the Commonwealth. These walls for many years served as a communication between the northern and western parts of the town ; but in 1835 the more modern portion was nearly buried in the formation of a new road.

R

RECREATIVE.

***

THE THEATRE.

WHEN man is contemplated in the character of a being, who can be successfully addressed by an appeal to the passions and the understanding, the Drama, under proper restrictions, may be rendered serviceable.

> I have heard
> That guilty creatures, sitting at a play,
> Have, by the very cunning of the scene,
> Been struck so to the soul, that presently
> They have proclaim'd their malefactions.
>
> SHAKSPEARE.

The old building used for the purpose of dramatic performance in this town, is said to have formed part of a royal dwelling of the Princes of Powys Land. Having long been ruinous, it was purchased by Mr. Bennett, the manager, and taken down in 1833. The erection of the present theatre on its site has been an important improvement to the thoroughfare leading to St. John's Hill and the Quarry, as well as an ornament to the town. It forms a centre and two wings; the lower part consists of a rusticated base, upwards of 100 feet in length, fitted up as shops, with a house for the manager. Above is a continued string-course, from which rises two pilasters in each wing, supporting a frieze and cornice.

The windows are finished with architraves, and the front of the building displays three niches, containing statues of the immortal bard SHAKSPEARE and of the COMIC and TRAGIC MUSE, executed in compos by Mr. James Parry a native of this town.

The interior of the theatre is conveniently arranged: in the centre is a dome, and the ceiling richly decorated with appropriate devices. The building is creditable to the taste of Mr. Bennett, whose spirited undertaking in this public improvement will no doubt be appreciated by the lovers of the drama. The new structure was opened Sept. 8th, 1834, under the patronage of the Mayor.

THE CIRCUS

is a large brick building near the Welsh bridge, in which

equestrian performances occasionally take place. It is used on fair days as a butter and cheese market.

THE HORSE RACES

are annually held in the third week of September, and continue for three days. They are generally attended by the rank and fashion of the county, and attract a considerable influx of visitors to the town. The king contributes a plate of one hundred guineas.

THE ASSEMBLY ROOM

was erected in 1777, at the back of the Lion Hotel, and is a commodious and tastefully decorated apartment, where most of the balls are held.

THE SHREWSBURY HUNT

takes place about the middle of November, and brings to the town a respectable number of the nobility and gentry of the county, who pass a week with a president annually chosen from the members, while a fashionable ball gives additional hilarity to the meeting.

ANGLING.

The Severn has long been celebrated for the excellency of its fish—salmon, pike, grayling, trout, perch, and many others. The votaries of the "Gentle Craft," if not always gratified with excellent sport, or the finny tribe should sometimes not be disposed "to bite," may find pleasure in the contemplation of the scenery around.

It must however be mentioned, and with regret, that the fishing of the river near the town has of late years been almost ruined by the daring excess of poaching with illegal nets, so as to threaten, as it were, the annihilation of the piscatory race, unless the laws are put in force for their defence. Some of the lesser streams near the town, however, afford a tolerable supply of good trout.

AQUATIC EXCURSIONS.

Much pleasant exercise and amusement is afforded on the Severn during the summer months. Several parties possess boats, and an emulation of skill is frequently excited among the more experienced rowers.

An annual gala is generally given by the young gentlemen of Shrewsbury School in the month of June.

Boats may be hired for the day at a moderate charge, and pic-nic parties take an excursion up the river to the picturesque and woody banks at Shelton, the shady groves near Berwick and the Isle, or downwards to the rural villages of Uffington, Atcham, &c. On a summer's evening, when all is calm and serene, the sail is truly delightful.

THE SUBURBS OF SHREWSBURY

comprise five separate districts, viz. Coton Hill, Castle Foregate, Frankwell, Abbey Foregate, and Coleham, containing a population equal to that within the walls.

In noticing these, it is purposed to commence where our walk terminated without the walls, viz. the Castle Gates, from whence the Castle Foregate and Coton Hill diverge. Taking the latter thoroughfare, to the left we enter Chester Street, into which a new line of road is opened, communicating with Mardol, and carried over the ancient fosse and through a portion of the wall erected by Robert de Belesme. A few yards further are

THE WATER WORKS,

which supply every house in the remotest part of the town with water for domestic purposes, being raised from the river by means of a steam engine, capable of throwing up 22,000 gallons in the hour. The Company was established under an act of parliament in 1830.*

Nearly opposite are

THE ROYAL BATHS,

* The town is supplied with most excellent water for drinking from a spring called Broadwell, which rises near Kingsland, and is conveyed by pipes under the river to a reservoir in one of the lodges at the principal entrance to the Quarry Walk, being conducted from thence to conduits placed in different parts of the town for the convenience of the inhabitants.

affording conveniences equal to any which are to be found
in the first-rate establishments of this kind in the kingdom,
while the moderate terms and strict attention to cleanliness
and comfort will, no doubt, ensure to them the patronage
and support of the public. Hot air, vapour, shower, warm,
salt, medicated, and fresh water baths are in constant readi-
ness, and the pleasure bath is of sufficient dimensions to
enable persons to learn the art of swimming.

The building is of a chaste design, the front being
ornamented with a portico, supported by two Ionic pillars
and two pilasters.

From the road, winding on the banks of the river, an
imposing view of the town may be obtained, with a considerable portion of the walls by which it was formerly
encompassed. A bold clump of trees on the right denotes

BENBOW HOUSE,

where the gallant Admiral Benbow was born in 1650, whose
distinguished deeds in arms have rendered him an honour
to our town and country. This brave sailor not only stood
against the enemy in the memorable action off Carthagena,
in August, 1702, until every hold was gone, but had to
encounter the unparalleled treachery of those under his
command. The operation of amputating his leg, which
was shattered by a chain-shot in the late engagement, added
to the deep mental anxiety occasioned by the base conduct
of his captains, brought on a fever which terminated his
career of glory November 4th, in the same year, universally
lamented. His remains received the rites of sepulture in
Kingston church, Jamaica.*

In the year 1828, a subscription was commenced in
this town for the purpose of erecting some memorial in

* A detail of the Admiral's splendid services will be found in the
" Biographia Britannica," and other similar works.

St. Mary's church (the parish in which he was born) commemorative of this distinguished Salopian, towards which
our no less courageous towsman, Admiral Sir Edward
Owen, K.C.B. with that frankness and honourable feeling
so characteristic of the true British sailor, munificently
contributed.

We now arrive at

COTON HILL,

where stood the suburban mansion of the Myttons of
Halston, in which that family resided after vacating their
town house of Vaughan's Place.   North-west of the turnpike was

ST. CATHARINE'S CHAPEL,

in a pasture still called the Chapel Yard.*

Coton appears at a remote period to have been connected with the Suburb of Frankwell by a bank, which
caused the river to spread over the meadows called the
" Purditches," forcing its waters from thence under Hencot
and Cross Hill in a channel still strongly marked by its
rising banks, and discernible at all times, especially during
floods, until the stream found its way into the present channel near the Royal Baths.   This is particularly evident at
the foot of Cross Hill, one mile on the Ellesmere road, to
the right of which a toll bar communicates with a pleasant
lane, the ancient road to Berwick.   From the brow of this
lane, the old course of the Severn may be easily defined.
From hence, also, the town unfolds itself with peculiar
beauty backed by the frontier of Salopian and Cambrian

* To the left of the turnpike is the Baschurch road, on which, at the
distance of one mile, are the beautiful Gates leading to Berwick House; a
short distance beyond is the neat structure of Berwick Chapel, re-built at the
close of the 17th century.—The town may be regained by a walk through
Almond Park, rich in sylvan beauty.

mountains, increasing in variety and picturesque effect throughout this delightful rural walk, until we arrive at Marshall's Factory, where a wooden bridge over the canal conducts again to the suburb of

THE CASTLE FOREGATE,

the point from which we at first diverged. This long street has become a place of much traffic, owing to a communication having been opened, in 1835, with Birmingham, London, Liverpool, &c. by means of THE SHREWSBURY CANAL, to and from which places goods are received into warehouses erected on its banks. This canal was originally formed in 1797, for the purpose of supplying the town and neighbourhood with coal, brought from Hadley, Ketley, &c. in the eastern part of Shropshire.

The canal terminates on the N. W. side of the County Prison, in a spacious

COAL WHARF,

belonging to the Canal Company, where this indispensible necessary of life may be obtained, of excellent quality, at fifteen shillings per ton. Coal is also procured at the collieries of Welbatch and Uffington, three miles distant from the town.

THE SUBURB OF FRANKWELL,

anciently written *Frankville*, lies on the west side of the Welsh bridge, and is a township within the parish of St. Chad. In former times it suffered much from the ravages of the Welsh, being in the line of road to the principality, as it is now the thoroughfare to Holyhead.

The inquisitive eye of the antiquary will discover in this suburb many curious specimens of the half-timbered dwellings of our ancestors, one in particular, better known now as the "String of Horses," appears, from initials, &c.

over the chimney piece, to have been erected at least as early as 1576. To the left of this building is "New Street," leading to Millington's Hospital, Kingsland, &c. Roads also branch off to the village of Hanwood, and the mining districts of Pontesbury and Westbury.

Passing onward to the right is St. George's church (page 89), a short distance from which is the "Mount," so called from a strong outwork erected during the civil wars, under the direction of Lord Capel, and in which he planted several pieces of cannon to protect the town. The garrison of this fort vigorously resisted the attacks of the parliamentarians, even after the town and castle had been captured. In the evening, however, of that day, they had no other alternative but to surrender upon bare quarter.

Near this fortification stood a religious house called Cadogan Chapel, which, in the third year of Edward VI. passed into lay hands. In 1604 it was remaining, though in a ruinous state, having been appropriated in that year as the "Pest House."*

The precinct of this chapel probably extended as far as Millington's Hospital, the site of the latter being to this day called "The Chapel Yard," and in the gardens adjoining it skeletons have been found, while a strong yew-tree hedge, still visible at the western end of Cadogan Place, was no doubt its boundary in that direction, near which spot stood "*Cadogan's Cross*," where sermons in other days were occasionally delivered. The bailiffs' accounts, for 1542, record the item of sixpence for wine given to the Lord President's chaplain, preaching at Cadogan's Cross on the Rogation day.

---

* In 1604 a great plague began in Salop, on the 2d of June, and raged until April following, in which time 667 persons had died of it in the several parishes, and the streets were so little frequented as to be covered with grass. The two bailiffs died.—MS. Chronicle.

The meadows below (on the banks of the Severn), called "*Monks Eye*," were granted by Reginald Pinzun to the "Almonry" of Shrewsbury Abbey, in the reign of Henry III. previously to which they bore the appellation of "*Crosfurlong*."

Extending our walk for one mile on the great Holyhead road (with the fine woods of Berwick on the opposite side of the river) we reach the township of SHELTON, where are some neat suburban villas which unite architectural taste and rural decoration with beauty of situation and commanding prospects. At this place stands

GLENDOWER'S OAK,

famed from the tradition that Owen Glendower, in 1403, ascended its branches to ascertain the event of the Battle of Shrewsbury, a circumstance not unlikely when it is considered that the country was probably more open at that time than at present.

This champion of Welsh independence, it has been already shown, assembled his forces at Oswestry, from whence, according to Holinshed, he sent off only his first division, consisting of 4000 men, who behaved with spirit in the day of action. The Welsh historians, however, have censured his conduct on this occasion, and blame him for what it appears from some cause he was unable to effect, viz. in neglecting to attack Henry after the battle, when the royal forces had sustained a severe loss and were overcome with fatigue, and when his own followers and the remainder of the northern troops would have formed an army nearly double that of the king's.

There are documents to prove that this oak was "*a great tree*" within 140 years after the Battle of Shrewsbury, and was an object of remark to old people long before. It is now a chronicle to the eye of the passing traveller, and to those who delight to be carried back into the depth of antiquity. Long may it be preserved from injury, and viewed as the natural historical monument of our vicinity; for Time has truly

> Hollowed in its trunk
> A tomb for centuries; and buried there
> The epochs of the rise and fall of states,
> The fading generations of the world,
> The memory of man.

According to a recent measurement, the tree is $41\frac{1}{3}$ feet in height; the girth at the base is $44\frac{1}{4}$ feet, and at eight feet from the ground $27\frac{1}{4}$ feet.

The interior is hollow, consisting of little more than a shell of bark, forming an alcove capable of holding a dozen individuals; and notwithstanding the branches of this aged tree have borne the blast of many a wintry storm, still it may be said—

> The Spring
> Finds thee not less alive to her sweet force
> Than the young upstarts of the neighbouring woods,
> So much thy juniors, who their birth received
> Half a millennium since the date of thine.

THE ABBEY FOREGATE.

Passing over the English, or east bridge, from which there is a striking prospect of the town and the tower on the Castle Mount, we reach a small tract of ground, comprising a few houses, called

MERIVALE,

or, *Murivale*, probably from its connexion with the walls.

In reference to this it appears that in the early part of the 13th century, the abbot consented that the two plats of ground between the main road at the east end of the bridge should be left void for the purpose of erecting defences in the time of war; hence Merivale subsequently became matter of frequent contest between the Corporation and the Abbey, as to the right of jurisdiction within it. This was not finally settled until the dissolution of the monastery, when Henry VIII. stating the "intimate affection" which he bears towards the town of Salop, and his desire "to do and shew favour to the bailiffs and burgesses," grants that they and their successors may for ever enjoy all the liberties, privileges, &c. within the limits of the Abbey Foregate, including the hamlet of Merivale, in as ample manner as they were enjoyed by the last abbot or his predecessors.

Leaving the National School to the right,

THE MONASTIC REMAINS

next claim our notice, and although now very inconsiderable, yet, like most other Abbeys, they originally consisted chiefly of two quadrangular courts of different dimensions, the conventual church, as was customary, being towards the north. Situated on the other sides were the refectory, almonry, chapter house, dormitory, locutory or parlour, infirmary, guest hall or hospitium, kitchen, and other domestic offices. The abbot's house or lodging commonly formed one or more portions of the smaller quadrangle, and consisted of a complete mansion.

This Abbey, bereft of its endowments by the reforming spirit of Henry VIII. shared the fate of other similar foundations in the rapine of the dissolution; the buildings connected therewith were sold, and soon afterwards despoiled of their constituent parts, chiefly for the value of the materials, while portions were converted into dwellings and other purposes, or left quietly to moulder into decay.

Of the remains which have excited most attention is an elegant octagonal

STONE PULPIT,

from which one of the junior monks was accustomed to read to his brethren while seated at their meals. Its situation, one half resting on the ruined wall of the Refectory, indisputably proves this ; looking outward of the site of that building it forms a small bay window, while the other portion, once inside the hall, is supported on a moulded bracket, which springs from a corbel originally carved as a head. From hence it projects to the basement of the floor, twelve feet from which rises a conical roof sustained on six narrow pointed arches, having trefoil heads.

The interior forms a beautiful oriel, the roof being vaulted on eight delicate ribs, at the intersection of which in the centre is a boss of comparatively large dimensions ; on this is beautifully sculptured The Crucifixion, with St.

John and the Virgin Mary at the foot of the cross, enclosed under a trefoil arch flanked by buttresses. The spaces of the three northern arches, looking inwards, are filled with embattled stone panels about three feet high, on which are enshrined several figures of saints, &c.

This interesting relic is approached from the garden by a flight of steps through a small doorway worked originally, it is considered, within the thickness of the wall of the refectory.

The south wing of what is supposed to have been part of the monk's infirmary, chapel, &c. remains south-west of the church. It is now appropriated as a malthouse, and may be distinguished by its lofty gables. A similar building converted into dwellings stood near the street, and was connected with the above by an embattled ruin flanked by massive piers, between which were square windows divided by a transom. This was an imposing feature to our monastic remains, and truly venerable from its antiquity, having braved the storms and tempests of nearly one thousand years, but was taken down without a feeling of forbearance in 1836, and the materials applied for the foundations of two houses adjoining its site.

The present Abbey house is supposed to have been the guest hall, or hospitium, to the east of which three pointed arches, once forming part of a groined ceiling, denote the abbot's lodging.

Of the chapter house, where the members of the monastery assembled to transact their official business, not a relic is left; but in excavating near its site, in 1836, a leaden seal was found, which had been once appended to a bull from the Pope, whose name is thus inscribed on it, INNOCENTIVS. PP. IIII.

The monks of this Abbey, in the third year of Pope

Innocent IV. i.e. 1246, obtained a bull, setting forth the injuries committed against their lands, tithes, possessions, &c. by the monastery of Lilleshall, by which the dean and precentor of Lichfield were directed to convoke the parties and hear the cause.

The dormitory was attached to the south-west side of the church, and was cut through in the formation of a new line of road in 1836.

What a train of reflections, loudly bespeaking the vicissitudes of life, may be called forth during our walk along this new thoroughfare. Who is there, it may be asked, with a mind to think and a heart to feel, that can thoughtlessly pass over ground which has been distinguished in history, without a momentary reflection upon its former importance?

Within the Chapter House, which stood on a portion of this road, occurred the earliest authorized assembly of that popular representation in the constitution of this kingdom, to which, under Providence, Englishmen have been indebted for all their subsequent prosperity,—all their energies, and that noble independence which have characterized us as a people among nations.*

Here, too, Richard the Second gratified his fondness for magnificence, by entertaining the members of his parliament with a sumptuous feast, and, as if to dazzle by the splendour of monarchy, and to awe by military display, he was attired in his royal robes, and attended by a numerous guard of Cheshire men.

The fervent orisons of a grateful heart have here been uplifted—divinity and other important subjects discussed—and on this spot the nobility, gentry, abbots, priors, deans, &c. of Shropshire, have frequently congregated, and banished for a time the gloomy silence and sable garb of the brother-

* Vide page 6

hood, and exchanged the sober gravity of the refectory, and its austere monkish repast, for wine and wassail, minstrelsey and song.

Before quitting these scattered ruins, the present remains of the Abbey church must excite feelings of regret in the breast of every admirer of our ancient architecture, at the mistaken zeal which caused its partial and barbarous demolition.

An embattled wall encompassed the northern and eastern sides of the precinct, beyond which is the FORE-GATE, a respectable open street, nearly one mile in length, and chiefly occupied by private residences. The houses to the south have gardens which extend to the Reabrook, and command delightful prospects of the adjacent country. This suburb (April 1st, 1774) suffered considerably from a fire, which destroyed 47 dwellings, 16 barns, 15 stables, 4 shops, and several stacks of hay, beside damaging other property.

On the left, half way up the street, is

THE WHITE HALL,

So called from a practice, during the last century, of occasionally colouring its deep red walls. Our native poet (Churchyard) speaks of this stone mansion in his usual quaint manner, as standing "so trim and finely that it graceth all the soil it is in." In front is a handsome gate-house; and the pointed gables, central cupola, and ornamental chimnies, strongly characterise it as an interesting specimen of the old English residence peculiar to the reign of Elizabeth, while its sombre appearance is finely set forth by the vivid foliage of walnut and other trees adjoining. The interior has been modernised, and forms a comfortable habitation. The building was commenced in 1578 by

Richard Prince, Esq. a celebrated lawyer, and was his manorial residence. It now belongs to the Right Rev. the Bishop of Lichfield, by purchase from Earl Tankerville.

A few yards distant is

THE RACE GROUND,

called the "Soldier's Piece," from the circumstance of Charles the First having drawn up his army here (page 11).

Situated within a very few minutes' walk of the town,

it may in most points compete with all the secondary courses in the kingdom. It is one mile and 185 yards in circumference, and in addition to a fine straight run for coming-in of 500 yards, possesses the advantage of a sight of the horses throughout the race, combined with an extensive panoramic view of the adjacent richly diversified country; while the town, from so many points picturesque, has from hence a most pleasing appearance.

It may be remarked that this race course is formed on a plan, it is believed, not previously adopted, the arrangement being such as to provide for any distance, from half a mile to four miles, the different lengths being conveniently fixed and marked with letters on short posts inside the course; a reference to which is placed in the winning chair for the information of the public.

A footpath through the meadows near the Hall conducts to the east end of Abbey-foregate, and the noble Column erected on the great London road in commemoration of the military achievements of Lord Hill, who, on his return to his native county, in 1814, was welcomed into Shrewsbury by his countrymen with all the splendid honours attendant upon a triumphal hero. The most enthusiastic rejoicings took place, and upwards of 20,000 persons assembled to witness the festivities, &c. provided on the occasion in the Quarry.

Leaving the venerable church of St. Giles to the left, and proceeding about one mile to the right, along a pleasant walk embellished throughout by an interesting prospect, we reach the saline and chalybeate spring called

SUTTON SPA,

situated in a retired dell near the margin of the Reabrook, and the property of the Right Hon. Lord Berwick.

The spring issues from a rocky stratum of ash-coloured

clay, or argillaceous schistus. The water is colourless, and exhales a faint sulphureous smell, much more perceptible in rainy weather. It has been compared with the Cheltenham water, but in reality bears a stronger affinity to sea water, possessing, however, an advantage over that in containing iron. In those cases, therefore, for which sea water is usually recommended it has been found most beneficial, and proves highly serviceable in the treatment of glandular affections, scrofula, and other diseases of the skin. A tumbler glassful operates as a brisk aperient.

The following analysis of the water was recently read at one of the scientific meetings of the Shropshire Natural History Society :—

Eleven cubic inches of the water contain about half a cubic inch of carbonic acid, partly free and partly in a combined state, a quarter of a cubic inch of atmospheric air, and a trace of sulphuretted hydrogen.

Sixteen fluid ounces contain of—

Iodine and bromine, each a trace
Carbonate iron, about 0.7 grain
———— lime and siliceous earth, each a trace
Anhydrous muriate magnesia, 8.8 grains
———— ———— lime, 30 grains
———— ———— soda, 121.3 grains.*

The importance of this spring is generally acknowledged, and it is matter of regret that proper accommodations for the advantageous use of the water have not been more effectually provided. A stone cistern, within a little shed, is the only receptacle for the water, the refuse from which, after being confined within a covered drain for a few yards,

* Pure muriate of soda does not contain any water in its crystallized state except what lodges in the interstices of the crystals, therefore the weight of that, as it exists in the water, would not exceed the weight above given; 30 grains muriate of lime indicate 51 grains crystallized muriate, 8.81 grains muriate magnesia indicate $15\frac{1}{2}$ grains.

flows into the brook, and has produced an artificial morass, whose surface (from the deposition of iron oxyd) is covered with an ochery scum.

The care of the spring and baths is entrusted to the occupier of a cottage on the spot.

On an elevated situation in an adjoining meadow stands the primitive parish church of Sutton, a characteristic specimen of the little Norman churches erected in villages. The west front is crowned with a cupola, and displays a modern window, but those on the other sides of the fabric are of the earliest kind, narrowing towards the exterior surface of the wall. The town may be regained by different routes over the meadows, which lead to

THE SUBURB OF COLEHAM,

situated on the southern banks of the river, where the Meole or Rea brook joins the Severn. This was until the present century the lowest part of the town, and consequently most liable to be inundated by floods; but of late years the street has been raised about nine feet.

The township is populous, and consists of two districts, called Longden Coleham and Meole Coleham from their respective thoroughfares to those villages. In the latter direction is Trinity Church, and in the former the extensive foundry of Mr. Hazledine, where the iron-work used in the construction of that surprising proof of human ingenuity, the " Menai Bridge," was cast, and proved by an engine whose pressure was calculated at thirty-seven tons.

TRADE AND MANUFACTURES.

Our town for more than three centuries possessed almost exclusively the trade with Wales in a coarse kind of cloth called Welsh webs, which were brought from Merionethshire and Montgomeryshire to a market held here weekly. In reference to this, Camden, in his "Britannia," published in 1586, writes of Shrewsbury—"It is a fine city, well inhabited, and of good commerce; and by the industry of the citizens and their cloth manufacture and their trade with the Welsh, is very rich, for hither the Welsh commodities are brought as to the common mart."

The termination of this branch of commerce is an event of too much importance to be passed over   It is thus graphically alluded to by Messrs. Owen and Blakeway: "Every Thursday the central parts of the town were all life and bustle; troops of hardy ponies, each with a halter of twisted straw, and laden with two bales of cloth, poured into the Market-place in the morning, driven by stout Welshmen in their country coats of blue cloth and striped linsey waistcoats."

At two o'clock the drapers, with their clerks and shearmen, assembled under the Market-house, and proceeded up stairs (according to ancient usage) in seniority. The market being over, drays were seen in all directions conveying the cloths to the several warehouses, and more than six hundred pieces of web have been sold in a day. The whole was a ready money business; and as the Welshmen left much of their cash behind them in exchange for malt, groceries, and other shop goods, the loss of such a trade to the town may be easily conceived. This took place about the year 1795, and was occasioned by individuals (not members of the Shrewsbury fraternity of drapers) travelling into those parts where the goods were made, from which the manufacturers soon learnt that they might find a mart for their goods at home without the trouble and expence of a journey to the walls of Amwythig.   In March, 1803, the company relinquished the great room over the market-hall, where they had for nearly two centuries transacted their business, and though much traffic in flannels was subsequently carried on in the town, the total extinction of this branch of our local commerce is fast approaching, from the market having diverged to Welshpool, Newtown, and Llanidloes, where the advantages of machinery are now substituted for manual labour in its manufacture.

The cessation of the woollen market in this town has been ascribed to the improvement of the roads in Wales, which opened a more free communication to the interlopers of the Drapers' company; and this again afforded some compensation to the town for the loss of this branch of its trade. For if Shrewsbury was no longer the emporium of North Wales, it was becoming the centre of communication between London and Dublin; and the agriculture of the neighbourhood and the trade of the town received a new impulse from the vast increase of posting and stage coaches, but far inadequate to the advantage which it derived from its trade in Welsh woollens and the weekly visits of the Cambrian farmers.

That Shrewsbury, however, may reap the full benefit of its central situation as the great thoroughfare from whence all the roads into North Wales diverge, and being also the general market of the surrounding country, acknowledged to be one of the finest agricultural districts in the kingdom, it is highly expedient that our town should possess the advantage of a RAILWAY communicating with the great lines to Birmingham, London, Liverpool, &c.

Prospectuses have been issued showing the eligibility of the plan, and the position in which the trade and general intercourse of the town will be placed if unprovided with those facilities of cheap and expeditious conveyance enjoyed by other large towns; and when it is considered that a great portion of the provisions which supply the thickly-populated neighbourhoods of Wolverhampton, Bilston, Birmingham, &c. are purchased at our weekly markets and monthly fairs, and the deficient and expensive means of transit on this line, a Railway would produce incalculable benefit to the town by an increased traffic, and thereby contribute to reinstate it in that important situation which it once held as THE EMPORIUM OF NORTH WALES.

The chief manufactories at present are the extensive concern of Messrs. Marshall for thread and linen yarns, three iron foundries, and Messrs. Jones and Pidgeon's for tobacco and snuff. The vicinity being a good barley country, the malting business is carried on to a considerable extent, and divided among sixty maltsters. Glass-staining has been brought to the highest state of perfection in this town, completely disproving assertions made some few years since that the powers of this ancient science had then extended almost beyond the hope of eventual excellence. The gothic chain, however, which for so long a period had confined the mystery of this beautiful art, once, indeed, considered as entirely lost, has been effectively broken by our townsman, Mr. D. Evans, of whose productions our churches and many other ecclesiastical buildings and noblemen's mansions in different parts of the kingdom afford specimens, contending in effect with some of the finest works of the ancient masters.

Among the *delicacies* for which our town is so deservedly celebrated may be mentioned a most delicious CAKE,* of which but few strangers in passing through fail to partake, especially if they have read the encomium of the poet Shenstone :

> " For here each season do these cakes abide,
> Whose honoured names th' inventive city own,
> Rend'ring through Britain's isle Salopia's praises known."

SHREWSBURY CAKES appear to have been presented

* " Why, brother Wilful of Salop, you may be as short as a SHREWSBURY CAKE, if you please."—Way of the World, 1735, by W. Congreve.

to distinguished personages on their visit to this town as early as the reign of Elizabeth; and when their Royal Highnesses the Duchess of Kent and the Princess Victoria arrived here in 1832, they were graciously pleased to accept a box of them from the Mayor.

The Simnel made here is much admired, and great quantities of this kind of cake are prepared about the season of Christmas and Lent. The word is supposed to have been derived from the Latin *simila*, signifying fine flour; but the common tradition fixes its origin to a dispute between a man named "Simon" and his wife "Nell." One of them was desirous that the plum pudding should be baked, while the other insisted that it should be boiled: neither party being disposed to yield, it was therefore first boiled and afterwards baked (the processes that it now undergoes), and thus produced Sim-nell. The exterior crust, or shell (enclosing a compound of fruit) is hard, and deeply tinged with saffron.

The Shrewsbury Brawn is unrivalled, and has lately been patronised by His Majesty William the Fourth. Brawn is a Christmas dish of great antiquity, and may be found in most of the ancient bills of fare for coronations and other great feasts. " Brawn, mustard, and malmsey" were directed for breakfast during the reign of Elizabeth; and Dugdale, in his account of the Inner Temple Revels, states the same directions for that society. It is prepared from the flesh of boars fattened for the purpose.

Shrewsbury Ale has been commended from a remote period. *Iolo Goch*, the bard of Owen Glendower, eulogises the profusion with which " Cwrw Amwythig," or Shrewsbury Ale, was dispensed in the mansion of his hero at Sycarth, which he seems to have visited previously to the insurrection of 1400.

T

In the last century the properties of this beverage were thus extolled :—

> " Hops, Water, and Barley, are here of the best,
> Your March and October can well stand the test ;
> The body is plump, and the visage ne'er pale,
> That imbibes, or is painted, with *Shrewsbury Ale.*"

MARKETS.

The market days are Wednesdays and Saturdays. The former is small, but that on the latter day is well attended and abundantly supplied. In fact, few towns enjoy the advantage of a better or cheaper supply of meat, poultry, butter, vegetables, fruit, &c. But it must be confessed that many places of far less importance than the capital of Shropshire possess more suitable accommodations befitting the ample produce brought from the surrounding districts to its markets.

The space allotted for the sale of vegetables is in the spacious square opposite the County Hall, commonly called the " Green Market;" that for poultry, eggs, &c. on Pride Hill and in the Butter Cross. The shambles for butchers' meat is in a street called " the Double Butcher Row;" and in Fish-street, near St. Julian's church, are sheds and stands for the country butchers. The corn mart is held under the old market house.

THE FAIRS.

The fair for the sale of horses, cattle, butter, cheese, &c. is held on the second Wednesday in every month; and that for sheep and pigs on the preceding day. It has long been in contemplation to form a proper " Smithfield" for cattle, &c. which are now disposed of in the streets, much to the annoyance of passengers. The wool fairs are in July and August.

THE SEVERN.

This beautiful stream, the queen of rivers,—famed in British story and noticed by classic historians,—the theme of poets and the admiration of tourists, is next in importance to the Thames.

It rises in Plinlimmon mountain, Montgomeryshire, and pursues its course through that county, receiving in its meanderings numberless tributary streams, and presenting to proud Salopia the richest variety of picturesque scenery. After winding sixty or seventy miles through the centre of Shropshire, passing Worcester, &c. it at length becomes " a mighty river, potent, large," and empties itself into the Bristol Channel, fifty miles below Gloucester.

THE NAVIGATION OF THE RIVER

is free for barges from thirty to eighty tons burden, during the whole of its course throughout Shropshire, which are towed up the stream by horses belonging to a company; but the navigation is liable to interruption from high and rapid floods in winter, and occasional want of depth of water in summer.

ENVIRONS OF SHREWSBURY

Present an agreeable variety of pleasant drives and interesting walks, unfolding from most points some changing feature of landscape scenery, insulated, or grouped in picturesque masses, and interspersed with lofty hills, which afford an imposing back-ground to the town, producing a succession of rich and varied prospects calculated to interest the lover of nature, while the artist, the antiquary, the botanist, or the geologist, may find an ample field for the cultivation of their respective pursuits.

The limited plan of the present work will only admit of a very brief notice of some of those objects that might claim the attention of the enquiring stranger, or present themselves in the course of a drive.

BATTLEFIELD,

Three miles N.E. by N. of Shrewsbury. Perhaps few events, so recent and of such importance in the annals of our country, have left so few local traditions to awaken the dream of ancient chivalry as the Battle of Shrewsbury.

The site of this momentous conflict for the crown of England is no longer unenclosed, but seems thriving with the culture of centuries of peace. Some armour and military weapons occasionally turned up remind us of the event, or, but for the Church piously founded by King Henry the Fourth, in commemoration of his victory over Hotspur, Douglas, Worcester, and the rebel army, we might rejoice that the breath of tranquillity has hushed the tale of death.

The many associations, however, connected with this
event, are not easily banished from the mind during a visit
to this spot, particularly when it is considered that it afforded
matter for the classic pen of Shakspeare.

BATTLEFIELD CHURCH,

According to the foundation of King Henry the Fourth,
consisted of five secular canons, and among other endowments possessed the churches of St. Michael within the
Castle of Shrewsbury, and also St. Julian's, in the same
town. The clear annual revenues of the college at the
dissolution being £54. 1s. 10d. as stated by Tanner.

The fabric, dedicated to St. Mary Magdalene, stands in

the centre of a pasture field, and consists of a nave, chancel, and finely proportioned tower, crowned with eight pinnacles and a richly decorated frieze and parapet. The choral division, from the style of the windows, was undoubtedly erected in the time of the founder, and the western portion under the auspices of the Very Reverend Adam Grafton, Dean of the Collegiate Church of St. Mary, Shrewsbury, Archdeacon of Salop, &c. &c. a person of great eminence in his day, and who possessed much architectural taste. His name is inscribed on the east side of the tower as warden of the college in 1504. Length of the church, including the tower, 94 feet.

The roof of the nave and chancel having fallen in from decay early in the last century, the latter was restored and supported by four doric pillars. The interior is neat.

In the south wall is the piscina and the sedilia for the officiating priests. In one of these is a curious wooden figure, called " Our Lady of Pity." It represents the Virgin seated and bearing on her knees a dead Christ.

The eastern window is of five divisions, and contains some remains of the stained glass with which this church was once enriched. The other portion having been taken down during a repair of the fabric some years since, was either lost or destroyed, through the negligence of the person to whom it was entrusted.

The subjects comprised a history of the death of John the Baptist, with various portraits of the knights who fell on the King's side in the battle at this memorable place. The crowned heads of King Henry the Fourth and his Queen, the portraits of a bishop or abbot, and the head of John the Baptist in a charger, may yet be distinguished, and are tastefully pencilled. The red and yellow colours throughout are particularly vivid. A beautiful border of foliage, with a mutilated inscription, is at the base of the window.

At the east end of the north wall is a handsome florid gothic monument to the memory of the late John Corbet, Esq. of Sundorne, who died in 1817. The basement is after the model of an ancient altar tomb, from whence rises five pannelled buttresses with mouldings supporting the canopy, which consists of four pointed ogee arches crocketed and crowned with finials. The interior is a richly groined vault, and at the angles are small turrets. The whole is beautifully worked in grained free-stone from the neighbouring quarry of Grinshill.

The nave of the church is roofless : on each side are three elegant mullioned windows, with tracery of different devices. In the walls are corbels formed into grotesque heads, on which rested the timbers that supported the roof.

The shaft of the ancient font (sunk in the ground) stands at the north-east angle of the pointed arch which separates the nave from the tower. The second floor of the tower is singularly furnished with a fire-place, having a chimney formed within the thickness of the wall and opening outside beneath the belfry window.

A tabernacled niche above the chancel window contains the crowned statue of Henry the Fourth : the right hand once sustained a sword, and on the same side also hangs the scabbard.

The college stood at the east end of the church, the moat which surrounded it being still visible. Near this part is a field called the " King's Croft," in which were placed a portion of the royal army. The troops of Hotspur appear to have been chiefly stationed on the north side.

On the south side of the church is a small cemetery, in which is deposited the remains of the late Rev. Edward Williams, M.A. who for nearly half a century was the

Minister of this parish—loved and honoured by his flock as a spiritual father, and the remembrance of whose virtues and christian instruction still lingers like a lovely twilight. He died January 3d, 1833, aged 70 years.*

GRINSHILL

Is four miles distant from hence. The village is picturesquely sequestered beneath the extensive stone quarries, of which great use has been made in the bridges, churches, and public buildings of Salop. About the year 1630 a large stone building was erected at this place for the reception of the scholars under instruction at the Royal Free Grammar School during the time any contagious disorder might prevail in the town. It is now used as a private classical and commercial school.

HAWKSTONE,

Being six miles further in this direction, is consequently beyond the prescribed limit of my pen. I cannot forbear, however, to remark that the scenery in the park is truly grand, and the objects which meet the eye are varied and interesting, consisting of a succession of hills and dales, rocks and caverns, connected together in a comparatively small space. The walks are twelve miles round, and the

* Mr. Williams possessed acquirements of no ordinary description, and was an accomplished scholar. He had studied much of botany, was an excellent draughtsman, and in early life devoted considerable attention to the study of antiquities, particularly those connected with his native county. His collection of materials relating to the History of Shropshire were most extensive, and although he did not favour the world with any publication shewing the result of his researches, he has, nevertheless, left behind a surprising proof of his perseverance in original drawings of all the churches, parochial chapels, monastic remains, castles, monuments, and tablets, in Shropshire, besides sketches of most of the mansions of the nobility and gentry in the same county.

obelisk erected on the terrace of the park commands a prospect one hundred miles in diameter.

Amid this beautiful natural scene, the hand of art has introduced many interesting features calculated to interrupt for an interval the associations of the mind, that it might return with renewed vigour and fresh delight to the enjoyment of the more exalted feast of contemplative wonder, which nature has so lavishly bestowed on this elysian spot. The noble proprietor kindly permits visitors to gratify themselves with a walk over the grounds.

HAUGHMOND ABBEY,

Three miles north-east of the town, is approached from the Old Heath, by a road full of picturesque beauty. The vale is watered by the Severn, while swelling hills fill up the distance.

This monastery was founded in the year 1100 by William Fitz Alan, for canons regular of St. Augustine, and is situated on the side of a gentle eminence. The ruins form a most imposing object, and are of sufficient consequence to attract the steps of the pedestrian. Of the Abbey church few remains exist. The door which opened into the cloister is an elegant specimen of anglo-norman architecture.

THE CHAPTER HOUSE is almost in a perfect state of preservation : the front parallel with the cloister consists of a fine entrance through a circular arch, with a window in the same style on each side, divided into small lights. The shafts of these arches have canopied niches containing mutilated statues ; the angel Gabriel, St. Catharine, and St. John may yet be distinguished.

THE ABBOTT'S LODGING is in part standing, being beyond the cloister and refectory southward. There is likewise the shell of a noble hall, having very early mullioned windows, and a very large one at the west end, the tracery of which is destroyed. At the extremity of this was the great chamber, lighted by a beautiful bow window (probably a later addition), and divided into an upper and lower story.

On the north side of the Chapter House are two monumental stones: the largest indicates the death of John Fitz Alan, Lord of Clun, great-grandson of William, the founder of the monastery, and the least that of his wife Isabel, daughter of Roger Mortimer, Lord of Wigmore.

The revenues of this Abbey at the dissolution were, according to Speed, £294. 12s. 9d. The buildings were sold, and converted into a spacious mansion. Haughmond demesne comprises about 1100 acres, within which is situated the castellated MANSION OF SUNDORNE, the property of Mrs. Corbet.

South-east, clothed with masses of woody verdure, is

HAUGHMOND HILL,

the etymology of which is derived from *haut mont*, the high mount. An easy ascent from the abbey leads to the summit, from whence is a rich panoramic prospect over a portion of the fertile vale of Shropshire, with the lofty steeples of its ancient capital, and the blue mountains of Cambria in the distance.

A castellated turret is erected on a steep crag of the hill, down which the Scottish Earl Douglas leaped with his horse, on being closely pursued after his escape from the Battle of Shrewsbury, and received a severe injury. He was taken prisoner, but the king, in admiration of his valour, set him at liberty.

At the foot of the hill is

THE VILLAGE OF UFFINGTON,

which is delightfully situated, and affords many rural beauties. Here for a time the lover of nature may enjoy that calm delight which moves the soul to contemplation; and whilst the eye has been charmed with the prospect enjoyed from the summit of the adjoining eminence, the heart seems hushed to the noise of a populous town, and a feeling of tranquillity imperceptibly steals upon the mind, for which a cause can scarcely be assigned.

Parties from the town are often tempted by the beauty of the situation to make this place a holiday retreat, whose enjoyment is enhanced by the accommodations of a good inn, attached to which, above the banks of the Severn, is a pleasant bowling green.

The church, overshaded by two venerable yews, possesses a primitive simplicity, quite in character with the village.

THE VILLAGE OF ALBRIGHTON,

distant three miles N. E. of the town on the Chester road. is a township in the parish of St. Mary, Shrewsbury. The church, a small humble structure, has been so effectually repaired by the modern goths with red stone and brick, that no reasonable conjecture can now be formed as to the period of its erection. A wooden loft issues from the west end, and inside the building is a curious ancient font, that will admit of total immersion, which has no doubt stood here for several centuries.

The fine old mansion near the church was formerly the residence of the ancient family of Ireland, who purchased this manor* on the dissolution of Shrewsbury Abbey.

A bridle road across a field leads to Albright Hussey and Battlefield. The former was the moated mansion of the Husseys, Barkers, and Corbets, but is now converted into a farm house. Here was a chapel, dedicated to Saint

* Etbrighton, a Saxon manor in Domesday.

John the Baptist, as appears by the grant of the land on which Battlefield church stands from Henry IV. to Roger Ive, of Leaton, who is there described as rector of the chapel of St. John the Baptist at Albright Hussey, and which chapel was by the said grant for ever annexed to the collegiate church of Battlefield; and Richard Hussey and his heirs were to be perpetual patrons of the same. The only vestige of the chapel is an old arch in a barn called the "chapel barn."

THE VILLAGE OF MEOLE,

otherwise Meole Brace, is one mile south of the town.* The church stands on a little knoll above the Rea brook, and was erected on the site of an ancient edifice in the year 1800. It is a plain cruciform building, with a tower rising from the roof at the west end.

From this place many agreeable walks branch off in the direction of Kingsland, Sutton, and the Sharpstones. Near the latter place, at Bayston Hill, is an earthwork of an irregular form, which seems to have been surrounded on all sides but the east by two fosses, the abrupt formation of the ground in that direction rendering such a protection unnecessary. The entrance was no doubt from the Stretton road at the west. The *double* entrenchment admits a probability that it belonged to the Anglo-Saxons, but it is

* Mr. Thomas Barker, author of a work on angling, was born at this village. From the singular vein of humour which runs through his book, he appears to have been a good-humoured gossipping old man. In the dedication he states, " I have written no more but my own experience and practice, and have set forth the true ground of angling, which I have been gathering these three-score years ; having spent many pounds in the gaining of it, as is well known in the place where I was born and educated, which is Bracemeale, in the liberty of Salop, being a freeman and burgess of the same city."—' Barker's Delight, or the Art of Angling,' was published a few years after Izaak Walton's Complete Angler (1659), to which Mr. Barker appears to have contributed the greater part of what is said on Fly Fishing.

difficult to distinguish between their encampments and those of the Danes, both forming their camps nearly alike and on elevated spots. The present site possesses every advantage for a military post of observation to the adjoining country. The residents in the vicinity designate it by the common appellation of the " Buries," and which appears to have escaped the notice of former topographers.

Two miles beyond this spot is the pleasant

VILLAGE OF CONDOVER.

The church is a spacious building, displaying examples of early Norman architecture. It contains several handsome monuments in memory of the ancient family of Owen, among which one from the chisel of Roubiliac is considered a remarkably fine production. The adjoining mansion, a most interesting specimen of the Elizabethan style of building, was erected by Sir Thomas Owen, Lord Chief Justice of the Court of Common Pleas, who died in 1598. Within the hall is the finest collection of paintings in the county. This village was the birth-place of Richard Tarlton, the earliest English comedian of celebrity, who for his surprisingly pleasant extemporaneous wit, as an actor and jester, was the wonder of his time. Fuller states, that " when Queen Elizabeth was serious and out of good humour, he could undumpish her at his pleasure." After a free and eccentric life, it is said he died penitent in 1588.

PITCHFORD,

six miles south-east of the town, takes its name from a kind of mineral pitch, which exudes out of a red sand stone, from which an oil is extracted called British oil. A similar substance is also found at this place, floating on a spring of water. Pitchford Hall is a beautiful specimen of the half-timbered mansion erected during the sixteenth century, and is the property of the Right Hon. the Earl of Liverpool, a descendant maternally of the Ottley family, one of whom purchased the estate in 1473.

The church, erected in the reign of Henry I. is a specimen of the lesser Anglo-Norman edifices erected in villages. Its foundation throws some light on the formation of our parochial establishments and the nature of tithes.

It appears that previously to its erection the inhabitants of the lordship went to some of the surrounding churches to hear divine service and receive the sacraments, and gave their tithes where they chose. Many of them contributed their tithes to the dean and chapter of St. Chad, in Salop, on condition that they found a chaplain and clerk, who should perform service three times a week, and daily visit the sick and baptize infants; but these duties being much neglected, one Ralph lord of Pitchford, moved by " charity and zeal," built a church at his own expence, and formed a certain district as the boundary of the parish.

At the distance of somewhat more than a mile is

ACTON BURNELL.

The remains of the ancient castle, founded by Robert Burnell, Bishop of Bath and Wells, consist of a large building, with a square tower at each angle. To this place the parliament of Shrewsbury adjourned in 1283, where were passed (and received the royal assent) certain legislative regulations, and amongst these the act touching merchant debtors, called " Statutum de Mercatoribus," designated likewise the Statute of Acton Burnell. The church is cruciform, and in the pointed style of the fourteenth century, having a wooden tower in the centre. Near this village is the seat of Sir Edward Joseph Smythe, Bart. and the grounds of the park are beautiful and extensive.

THE VILLAGE OF ATCHAM,

Three miles and a half east of the town, is delightfully seated on the banks of the Severn, over which there is a handsome bridge of seven arches, designed by Mr. Gwyn, a native of Shrewsbury.

The etymology of the place seems to be derived from *Eatta*, a Saxon saint to whom the parish church is dedicated. It was anciently called Ettingeham and Attingesham. In the Saxon period it belonged to the college of St. Alkmund, Shrewsbury; and when that church was annexed to Lilleshull Abbey, the advowson of Atcham made part of the transfer.

The present edifice consists of a nave without aisles; the predominant styles of the windows may be attributed to the fifteenth century; some of them are decorated with stained glass. The interior contains monuments belonging to the family of Burton, of Longner, removed hither on the fall of St. Chad's church, Salop.*

The basement of the tower is early Norman, and flanked with broad shallow buttresses. The portal at the west is a deeply recessed round arch, resting on five slender pillars on each side; above is an early lancet window, over which is another of smaller dimensions, bisected by a short pillar into narrow lights. The superstructure of the tower (like

v 2

* Longner, the ancient seat of the Burtons, is about one mile N. W. of this village, and forms part of the parish of St. Chad. In 1558 it was the residence of Edward Burton, Esq. a zealous protestant, who expired suddenly with joy on hearing of the accession of Queen Elizabeth. His body was refused interment in the church of St. Chad by the popish priest, owing to some stipulations made either in his will, or by the zeal of his surviving friends, that the popish service should not be celebrated over his remains, which were in consequence buried in his own garden, over which a plain altar has been erected, with a quaint poetical inscription.

many others in the vicinity) is of the sixteenth century, and was once crowned with eight pinnacles, the remains of which are now only visible above the frieze of the battlements.

The village is remarkable as being the birth-place of Ordericus, the earliest Salopian historian. He was the son of Odelerius Constantius, of Orleans, a chief councillor to Roger de Montgomery, born (as he informs us) Feb. 16, 1075, " and on the Easter Sunday following was baptised by Ordericus the priest at Ettingesham, in the church of St. Eatta the Confessor," and received the rudiments of his education under Siward the priest, in the little church of St. Peter, Shrewsbury, on the site of which the stately Benedictine abbey was afterwards built. Ordericus's great work is entitled an " Ecclesiastical History," but is more properly a record of the events of his own time.

Atcham once had the privilege of a fair, and the inhabitants were styled burgesses.

Opposite the inn, a pleasant drive leads through the village of Uffington, by which Shrewsbury may be regained. Continuing our course for half a mile on the London road, we pass over TERN BRIDGE, below which the river Tern falls into the Severn. On the left, ATTINGHAM HALL, the elegant mansion of the Right Hon. Lord Berwick, with its lofty portico, forms a bold and imposing object, and its beautiful situation near the confluence of the rivers Tern and Severn, imparts an additional charm to the surrounding scenery. To the right is

WROXETER.

This village was the metropolis of the *Cornavii*, a tribe of Britons settled in Shropshire and some of the adjoining counties at the period when Julius Cæsar first invaded this island. On the subjugation of the Britons this place became the flourishing Roman station of Uriconium,—Wriconium, synonymous with the adjoining Wrekin,*—subsequently Wrekincester, and by contraction Wroxeter.

It is situated on a gentle eminence above the Severn, possessing those advantages which the Romans generally kept in view, viz. dryness of soil, extensive prospect, and the protection of a river. From the almost impenetrable obscurity in which its early history is involved, no adequate idea can now be formed of the pristine state of this interesting place.

The town was undoubtedly defended by a wall and ditch, the boundaries of which are still to be traced throughout a circumference of three miles.

According to the best writers, we find that the Romans entirely quitted Britain about the middle of the fifth century, on which the Britons continued to occupy this place (deserted by their former masters) until they were ejected from it by the superior force of the Saxons sometime in the following century, and obliged to find a retreat among " the alders and willows which hid the ˙foot and the thickets which crowned the summit of the peninsular knoll, now covered by the capital of Shropshire."

How long the fugitives remained at Caer Pengwern unmolested it is now in vain to enquire, but this appears certain, that they were soon followed thither by the unsparing Saxons, and compelled to seek another refuge in the mountain fastnesses of Wales.

There can be no doubt but the fall of Wroxeter was, as Leland asserts, " the cause of the erection of Shrews-

v 3

* A great battle seems to have been fought near this hill ; for in 1833 a quantity of spear heads and celts, formed of brass, or some other composition of copper, and of rather elegant workmanship, were found near the Wrekin Farm.

bury;" and from the blackness of the soil in some parts its
destruction seems to have been by fire; many of the coins
also, and other remains discovered here, exhibit marks of
their having been subjected to that element: in fact, the
savage ferocity of the Saxon conquerors in their warfare,
together with their ascendancy over the Britons, was so
determinate and effectual in the demolition of those stations
which they held, that little surprise need be excited so few
vestiges remain of the Roman provinces in this kingdom,
or of the many works of art which that nation doubtless
left on their departure.

The Saxons on their invasion wielded fire and sword
unsparingly. It was their practice, on gaining possession
of a town or city, immediately to level it with the ground;
and it is recorded, that one of these triumphant barbarians
boasted that in three days after he has gallopped his horse
without stumbling over the spot on which the captured
station stood.

Wroxeter will be regarded by the antiquary with curious attention, as affording matter of much investigation:
indeed it is impossible, even in imagination, to look upon
its fruitful fields, teeming in the rich luxuriance of culture,
—once covered with a flourishing Roman town,—now presenting only the ruined remnant of a wall, without sensibly
feeling the instability of human greatness, and exclaiming
with Cowper—

> We turn to dust, and all our mightiest works
> Die too. The deep foundations that we lay,
> Time ploughs them up, and not a trace remains.
> We build with what we call eternal rock :—
> A distant age asks where the fabric stood ;
> And in the dust, sifted and search'd in vain,
> The undiscoverable secret sleeps.

The ruined wall still remaining is about 70 feet long

and 28 feet high, and is composed of layers of rough stones and large flat tiles at alternate distances. It is arched, and the interior thickness is formed with rubble and small pebbles thrown in with the cement or mortar, which is become harder than stone. This venerable relic is thought to have been a portion of the fortification of the town. Other conjectures are, that it might have been connected with the Prætorium, or have been part of a bath, which was discovered at no great distance from it; but after a lapse probably of more than 1600 years, and where evidence is wanting to guide us, its original purpose must remain in uncertainty.

Tesselated pavements, sepulchral stones with inscriptions, urns, skeletons in deep graves and encased in red clay, several moulds for coining money, seals of different kinds, an Apollo (four inches in length) elegantly cast in lead, with other figures, and many curious and interesting remains of Roman manufacture, have been discovered whilst excavating on this site. A stone altar, found near the vicarage in 1824, is thus inscribed—

BONO REI

PVBLICAE

NATVS.

Great quantities of copper coins, and many of gold and silver, are constantly turned up by the plough. The copper coins are chiefly of the lower empire.

The town was situated on the line of the Watling Street road, in the direction towards Stretton. In the ford across the Severn the foundations of a bridge may be discerned at low water.

Near this spot a discovery was made at the end of the last century, which no doubt denoted the burial-place of some family of distinction resident at this colony. It consisted of an enclosure of large stones a little below the surface of the ground, within which were deposited three large urns composed of a beautiful transparent green glass, each having one handle elegantly ribbed, and severally containing burnt bones and a glass lachrymatory. Some earthen urns, an earthen lamp, and a few Roman coins, were also found at the same place, the whole being covered with large flat stones.

The village church, on the accession of Henry II. was granted to the canons of Haghmond Abbey, and is an edifice deserving of attention, displaying in its construction several specimens of architecture between the earliest Anglo-Norman and the incongruous reparations of the last century. The building consists of a nave and chancel ; in the latter is a curious doorway, and the former seems to have had originally a south aisle. The tower was probably erected in the reign of Henry the Eighth.

In the church are three handsome altar tombs, bearing full-length cumbent effigies of Lord Chief Justice Bromley, who died May 15, 1555, and Isabel his wife ; Sir Richarde Newporte, Knyghte (Queen's Counsel in the Marches of Wales), and Margaret his wife, only daughter of the Lord Chief Justice ; and John Berker, of Haghmond Abbey, Esq. and Margaret his wife, second daughter of Sir Francis Newport, Knt. who died in 1618.

In 1824 these were judiciously restored and beautified. In addition to which there are mural monuments, with inscriptions, commemorative of Francis, Viscount Newport and Earl of Bradford, who died Sept. 19, 1708 ; also the Hon. Andrew Newport, his brother ; and a tablet to the memory of Andrew Newport, *utter* barrister, who died in 1611.

The vicinity of Wroxeter affords a delightful display of pastoral beauty,—the bright river, with every other requisite for the finest landscape scenery.

Five miles distant is the famed Shropshire mountain,

THE WREKIN,

the proud monarch of the plain, whose bold arching head rises to the altitude of upwards of 1300 feet. A pathway from the London road leads through plantations to its summit, from whence the admirer of nature may luxuriate in the enjoyment of a magnificent prospect, whilst he contemplates all that variety of hill and dale, wood, rock and stream, studded with mansions and villages, stretched like a map throughout a circumference of nearly 400 miles.

This NATURAL HEART OF SHROPSHIRE forms a conspicuous feature in the landscape from all parts of the surrounding country ; while it is universally regarded, from the king in his palace to the peasant in his cottage, as the centre towards which the best wishes and affections of the heart converge, in that well-known convivial sentiment which possesses the advantage over other toasts,—in being old without age, inasmuch as it is unchanged by time, and never out of place—

" ALL FRIENDS ROUND THE WREKIN."

JOHN EDDOWES, PRINTER, SHREWSBURY.

A

DESCRIPTIVE ACCOUNT

OF

SAINT CHAD'S CHURCH,

SHREWSBURY;

AND THE SPLENDID

CHANCEL WINDOW

OF

Stained Glass,

(COPIED FROM THE CELEBRATED "DESCENT FROM THE CROSS,"
BY RUBENS, IN THE CATHEDRAL AT ANTWERP.)

BY

HENRY PIDGEON,

AUTHOR OF "MEMORIALS OF SHREWSBURY," &c.

SHREWSBURY:

PRINTED BY JOHN EDDOWES, CORN-MARKET.

MDCCCXLII.

THE additional enrichment of another of our Churches must be highly gratifying to every Salopian; and as our ecclesiastical edifices justly claim most especial admiration from all who visit them, and hold a pre-eminent feature of decoration above those of any town in the kingdom, it is to be desired that the suitability of their purpose will not be overlooked by those for whose particular benefit and accommodation they are intended.

The judicious reparation of the more ancient structures and the embellishment of the modern, has mainly been accomplished by an unostentatious and Christian-like munificence from private individuals,—probably unexampled in extent, and deserving to be had in lasting remembrance, as devoted to the honour of God, and rendered subservient to the noblest uses of mankind.

To give increased dignity to the Temple of that Supreme Being where his creatures worship is in accordance with a principle derived from a remote antiquity, that places for Divine adoration ought in their general appearance to be made worthy of the High and Holy purposes to which they are devoted. At the same time it is to be desired that the associations connected with this feeling will generate a desire for those sublime interests belonging to that Omnipotent Power to whose particular service and glory ecclesiastical architecture is dedicated; and that this will moreover dispose to refine the feelings, elevate the thoughts, and to correct that low and debasing view so truly of the "earth, earthy," in which religious observances even in this enlightened age are unfortunately too much regarded.

The evidence of history, both in the ancient as well as in the modern world,—in savage as well as in civilized nations—has exemplified the fact that architecture is indebted to almost every kind of religion for the most elaborate buildings, adapted as far as possible to the peculiar customs, rites, and economy of the people.

How far, however, architects during the past and preceding century have made their buildings either in form or character consonant with that awe and veneration which should distinguish the ceremonies of the Christian religion and the doctrines inculcated by its ministers, is too apparent to be equivocal in many otherwise fine structures in the metropolis and other places, which, if their towers or steeples be excepted, possess but little exterior token of religious appropriation.

The Church now under notice has thus called down
severe criticism from many, whose zeal in the condemnation
of novelty in the design, has hurried them not unfrequently
into an extreme of animadversion, quite contrary to the
sentiment which should, under any circumstances, harmonize with the spirit of that holiness to which the edifice
has been solemnly consecrated.

The rebuilding of St. Chad's Church was occasioned
by the fall of the old cathedral-like edifice, July 9th, 1788,
which occupied the southern eminence of the town.   It was
a spacious cruciform structure erected in the reign of
Henry III. on the site of a former edifice.   The only
portion now remaining was originally a Chantry Chapel
dedicated to the Virgin Mary, and, subsequent to the
Reformation, called the "Bishop's Chancel," from its
being used at the Visitations of the Bishop and Archdeacon.

That a circular plan was adopted in the New Church,
in preference to the lofty proportions of a design more
congenial to English feelings and prejudices is a circumstance much to be regretted.

This was the result of a misunderstanding on the part
of the architect, Mr. George Steuart, of London, with the
committee of parishioners chosen to manage the rebuilding.
The latter had been wearied in their endeavours by much
difference of opinion as to the eligibility of the old scite,
and further contention and delay in the selection of another
more suitable, while the former having completed estimates,
plans, working drawings, &c. adapted as he considered
under their approbation for land forming a portion of
the Quarry, would not prepare others until he was re-
munerated for those with which he understood them to be
satisfied.   The Committee being unwilling to cause a re-
newal of the angry disputes which the re-edification of

the Church on another spot had already produced, and to save time and expence, resolved, at a small meeting, to commence the new structure on the proposed circular plan, which took place March 2d, 1790, being the Festival of the Patron Saint, and, by active management, was completed and consecrated August 19th, 1792, the ground being held under lease from the Corporation of Shrewsbury for a period of 999 years, at an annual rent of nine pounds, ten shillings.

ST. CHAD'S CHURCH

Is erected on a most beautiful site near the Quarry, and considering the disadvantages of form which preclude the possibility of much architectural effect, may be looked upon as an ornamental building—being composed of fine Grinshill stone procured in the neighbourhood.

The Church is formed by the intersection of two circles, with a lofty tower and portico attached ; the smaller of the circles forming the inner vestibule containing the grand staircase, and the larger one the body, chancel, and side staircases leading to the gallery ; a portion of the circle inside being taken off for the latter purposes, which affords likewise a recess for the chancel. The basement of the tower is open, on each side of which is a square wing 24 feet by 19, appropriated as a vestry and a place for the transaction of parochial business.

The exterior is divided into two stories, the lower one being rusticated, and the upper springing from a moulding displaying a continued Ionic entablature, supported by coupled pilasters of the same order ; above the cornice is a well-proportioned balustrade, intended by the architect to have been crowned with statues of the twelve apostles.

The windows are circular headed in the upper, and square in the lower story, and, with the exception of that in the chancel, are uniform; the latter is Venetian, the divisions being formed with Corinthian pillars.

The portico consists of four Roman Doric columns and entablature in full order, and is considered a very fine specimen.

The steeple is divided into three parts, and, like the body of the church, is rusticated at the base, which is square; on this rests the second division, or bell chamber, octangular in shape, and decorated with Ionic pilasters, cornice, &c.; above rises eight elegant Corinthian columns, surrounded with an iron railing, and surmounted by a dome, cross, and vane.

THE INTERIOR carries with it an air of importance, grandeur, and extent, derived mainly from that form which in the exterior has so much shackled the efforts of the architect: dazzled for a moment by the first impressions, the detail is lost in the general effect; but from the whole the eye is directed to those parts which constitute that whole, and here defects may be discovered that will not stand the test of architectural scrutiny.

The seats are well constructed, every individual being able to see the officiating minister. The gallery is not thrown too forward, but is in every respect in unison with the size of the church; it is carried round the whole area with the exception of the chancel, and is supported by a double row of ill-proportioned Ionic columns, painted porphyry. A continued balustrade finishes the front of the gallery, from which rises slender fluted columns (surmounted with entablature) for the support of the roof, the frieze being decorated with angels, encircled by a glory within a wreath of honeysuckles. The ceiling is enriched with a large glory and cherubs in the centre, surrounded by a wreath and other devices.

This part of the building has recently undergone a great improvement, by means of a subscription promoted by Edward Muckleston, Esq. senior churchwarden. The ceiling with the entablature and frieze were originally of a cold white colour, and gave to the columns in front of the gallery an appearance of supporting nothing but plaster. This defect has now been remedied, the frieze, &c. being painted in imitation of oak, and the modillion cornice egg and tongue, and ogee mouldings, gilded.

It was the wish of several of the subscribers that the large centre glory should have been one mass of gold, but the taste of the decorator has, with more judgment, distributed the gold around the prominent parts of the entire cornice, and properly heightened the above ornament at the extreme points of the rays, preserving the same tint as in the ground of the ceiling, and shadowed from the clouds. This has produced an aerial effect, as well as an appearance of loftiness to the interior. The portions of the ceiling verging from the entablature are tinted darker to harmonize with the oak cornice, but proceed gradually lighter towards the centre.

The walls of the building are coloured of a much deeper tint than heretofore, which has added greatly to the solemnity of the interior, by giving it an air of repose, consistent with its sacred character.

The whole of the painting and decorations are highly creditable to the taste and judgment of our townsman Mr. T. Birch, to whom the committee of trustees left the whole management, a confidence, it is evident that has not been misplaced.

THE CHANCEL,

contrary to the general custom, is towards the North, and is separated from the body of the Church by a handsome arch springing from an entablature supported by coupled composite columns, elegantly proportioned, and the capitals richly gilt. The intrado of the arch is panelled, and in the apex, within a circle, is an open flower. Many additions have been made to this part in the way of decoration. The walls and ceiling (formerly white and of water colour) are painted porphyry, and the mouldings being relieved with gold, display to great advantage the several lines of the arched recess; the spandril between which, and the centre light of the window, contains cherubs, issuing from a mass of clouds and diverging rays, which are in solid gold.

The altar-piece is of oak wainscot, with panels inscribed according to the canon of the Church. These are surrounded by a deep border, which with the mouldings of the wainscot on the side walls and the rails in front of the communion, are gilded. Above is a large Venetian window, the divisions being formed by Corinthian columns at the expense of the the Rev. R. Scott;* these support a handsome cornice and architrave, the caps and finishings of which with the side pilasters are enriched with gold. This has given a bold and beautiful termination to the Church; and corrected the flat heavy appearance it formerly possessed.

This window formerly contained a painting in enamelled glass of the Resurrection of our Saviour, by the elder Eginton, but was replaced in the month of September, 1842, by the great munificence of the REVEREND RICHARD

---

* This gentleman, in the embellishment of the chancel and other gifts, including the splendid window, has expended the munificent sum of nearly £1500.

Scott of this town, with another in stained glass, from a copy of the celebrated painting by Rubens, in the South transept of the Cathedral at Antwerp, and for the reception of which the window of this Church is well adapted, both in form and size. The compartments, or auxiliary paintings even render the picture more interesting, these lateral divisions (or wings) in the original, forming folding doors to the principal subject, which were only opened on special occasions and festivals.

The centre compartment contains "The Descent from the Cross," and the side lights, "The Visitation" and "The Presentation in the Temple."

"The Descent from the Cross" is a painting, beyond all doubt, of extraordinary merit. In colouring, expression and design, nothing can exceed it as a composition. The pale, ghastly, and relaxed figure of the dead Christ is appallingly true to nature, and contrasts vehemently with the ardent expression and muscular energy of those who are supporting it ; while the hanging of the head on the shoulder, and the falling of the body on one side, give an appearance of the heaviness of death, passing description. It is more than a monitor to the feelings, for it speaks direct to the heart. The white drapery intended to cover the sacred body, and which extends downwards from the height of the cross, serves as a base to this noble figure, and relieves, by its clear mass of light, some of the predominant tints.

The grouping of the figures around the body of Christ is pyramidical, and displays the three Marys and five of the disciples, all zealously occupied in the same action—Solicitude, Love, and Grief. The beauty of Mary Magdalene is particularly striking, and upon whose shoulder the foot of our Saviour seems to rest. What grief pourtrayed in the countenance of Mary, the mother of Jesus !—full of tears and of sorrow, she raises the maternal hands, as if seeking to secure a sad and last consolation in the embrace of her Son and Lord, while the face appears radiant with a sweetly resigned and heavenly expression—a serenity that seems even imparted to those around her, and, most of all, in the tender attachment of the female at her side, who is gazing up at Christ with a look of intense anxiety.

These figures of the Marys, Sir Joshua Reynolds has remarked, have more grace than Rubens generally bestowed on female figures.

The disciples, leaning over the top of the cross, are in the act of lowering the blood-stained body, from the grasp of one of whom it appears as if just released. To the left, Joseph of Arimathea supports the drooping and declining body under the arm ; and Saint John, the beloved disciple, standing on the ground, and with one foot resting on the step of the ladder, is characteristically depicted as bearing in his arms the greatest burden of the hallowed remains.

The white sheet on which the corpse rests is, in contrast with the flesh, a bold effort (even in the copy from Rubens), being judiciously and skilfully used to sustain the essential unity and general harmony, by fixing the most clear and vivid light on the centre of the group, and by which means the colours acquire a fresh intensity, and secure successful opposition in the principal parts.

The *red* tunic of St. John, and the *green* drapery of Mary Magdalene, contrasted with the pale body of the Saviour, heighten the apparent projection in front, while the *blue* mantle of the Virgin Mary (half of which is in shade), the *blue* and *purple* tone of the vestments of Joseph of Arimathea, and of the disciple who is seen to the right, serves to round off the sides.

To the left of the spectator is "THE VISITATION OF MARY TO ELIZABETH." The history is recorded by the Evangelist Luke, i. chap. 39 verse, &c. "And Mary arose in those days, and went into the hill country with haste, into a city of Judah, and entered into the house of Zacharias, and saluted Elizabeth," &c.

This shows a landscape scene. The Virgin Mary and the female with a basket are supposed to be portraits of Rubens' two wives, while the figure denoting Joseph is said to represent the great artist himself.* Elizabeth and her husband are meeting them beneath a portico.

On the right is "THE PRESENTATION IN THE TEMPLE," and founded on the words of Holy Simeon, "Lord, now lettest thou thy servant depart in peace, according to thy word."

This is an excellent subject. The head of the Priest nothing can exceed: the expression, drawing, and particularly the colouring of the robe, are remarkably fine. Having blessed the Divine Infant, whom he holds in his arms, the venerable servant of God is in the act of returning him to his mother, whose hands are extended to receive her son. Joseph is kneeling in the foreground, and the aged Prophetess Anna, in the back ground, forms one of the group.

Such is a brief descriptive outline of what may be termed the poetical beauties of this celebrated picture, which, although beyond the power of posterity to approach

---

* Such is the common opinion. There is, however, a picture which adorns the altar in the Family Chapel of St. James, Antwerp, by Rubens, representing the Virgin Mary and the Infant Jesus, with the adoration of St. Bonaventura, which contains, besides the portraits of three females (two of them being his own wives), that of the artist himself, who is represented as St. George.

as a work of art, has nevertheless been admirably copied from the original at Antwerp by Mr. John Bridges, of London, for our townsman, Mr. David Evans, who has displayed his skill in delineating the subject in stained glass. This has been accomplished in a manner even to exceed the anticipations that were reasonably formed from the abilities he has already evinced in several masterly productions; and when the magnitude of the present subject, and the many casual difficulties he had to encounter, are taken into consideration, it will be found that the lights and shadows are distributed and managed with fidelity of effect and delicacy of touch,—that, as in the original painting, the eye is ever directed to the principal object.

It is somewhat difficult to write in terms which shall at once express the high character of the talent developed in this great undertaking, or the noble liberality of the Reverend Donor, which has called it forth, without almost offending by a semblance of unseemly commendation;—it may, however, be mentioned, that while the subject itself is the *chef-d'œuvre* of Rubens, so the taste and ability displayed in the execution of this window—added to the mellowed brilliancy of the glass—will stamp it as the finest production and boldest attempt of modern glass staining in the kingdom, and will prove Mr. Evans to be the *facile princeps* of modern artists in that department; at the same time it is to be hoped the work will remain for many generations as a striking memorial of individual munificence and individual taste.

HANC QUAM VIDES FENESTRAM AD EXEMPLAR
CELEBERRIMÆ ILLIUS PICTURÆ ANTVERPI-
ENSIS QUAM ACCURATISSIME ADUMBRATAM
D.D. RICARDUS SCOTT, S.T.B. E. COLL. ÆN.
NAS. APUD. OXON. AS. MDCCCXLII.

The foregoing inscription is placed at the base of the centre compartment of the window.

From this description it may be proper to mention the circumstances which gave rise to this wondrous effort of the pencil, which has conferred immortality on the name of the illustrious painter. It is said that Rubens in preparing the foundations of his new villa near Antwerp had by chance trespassed on some ground belonging to the company of Arquebussiers. A law suit was threatened, and Rubens, with all the vivacity of his nature, had prepared measures of resistance, but being assured by his friend Rockox, an eminent lawyer of the City, that the right was with his opponents, he gave way, and offered to paint a picture as a compromise. The offer was accepted, and the company required a representation of their Patron Saint "Christopher" to be placed in the chapel of the cathedral. Rubens presented to his adversaries not merely a single representation of the Saint, but an elaborate illustration of his name (the Christ bearing). Thus, in the centre, the disciples are lifting Christ from the cross and sustaining him in their arms; on the wings we have the Visitation—St. Simeon, with Christ in his arms, St. Christopher, with Christ on his shoulders, and the old hermit bearing the light. The Arquebussiers were at first disappointed not to have their Saint represented in the usual manner, and Rubens was obliged to enter into an explanation of his work, with which they were satisfied. Thus, without knowing it, they had received, (as it has been well remarked,) in exchange for a few feet of land, a miracle of art which neither money nor lands can now purchase. Louis XIV. wished to possess this picture, and employed the Marechal de Villeroi to treat with the city of Antwerp for the purchase ; but neither the influence of the "Grand Monarque," nor the offer of a sum of money enormous for that time, availed. To the credit of the merchant citizens, it is said, they rejected every temptation, and the King was obliged to content himself with a fine copy, painted for him by Gaspar Van Apstal in 1704.*

Peter Paul Rubens, considered as the Prince of Flemish Painters, was born at Cologne, 29th June, 1577. He shewed an early taste for literature, and was a person of much learning, sagacity, and knowledge, and acquired by his industry an immense fortune. He married Elizabeth Brant, daughter of a Magistrate at Antwerp, in November, 1609. She died 29th Sept. 1626. In 1631 he formed a second matrimonial alliance : his bride was Helena Forman, a beautiful lady of sixteen, belonging to one of the richest and most respectable families of Antwerp. Her portrait is found in many of his historical pictures. He received the honour of Knighthood from King Charles I. in 1630. The great artist died in 1640, in the 63d year of his age.

The pulpit and reading-desk stand in the middle of the area in front of the chancel. The organ is placed above the great entrance of the Church : it is in a mahogany case, having on the front a small painting of David playing upon the harp. The instrument was built by Gray, of London, and cost 400 guineas. The election of organist has been vested with the Corporation since 1713, who contribute £25 per annum towards the salary, in considera-

* A window in enamelled glass of "The Descent from the Cross," was executed by Mr. Muss, in 1824-5, for St. Bride's Church, Fleet-street. This does not give a perfect idea of the original picture. The whole of the light is thrown upon the body of our Saviour, while the rest of the painting is quite obscure, producing the sort of effect that Rembrant would have given to the subject had he treated it rather than that which Rubens has invested it. The fine group of women at the foot of the cross is quite undiscoverable.—*Vide* "*Churches of London.*"

tion of certain pews occupied by them in the Church. Between the piers of the gallery windows are hatchments, and the building, although of modern date, contains several tasteful mural monuments.

Among these may be mentioned a large panelled tablet, having a bust of the deceased by Chantrey, within a recess, commemorative of Mr. John Simpson, "who superintended the building of this Church; the bridges of Bewdley, Dunkeld, Craig, Ellachie, and Bonar; the aqueducts of Pontycysyllte and Chirk; and the locks and basins of the Caledonian Canal." He died in 1815, aged 60 years.

A similar one, with a bust by the same sculptor, on the corresponding side, is to the " Memory of Mr. William Hazledine, of this town, iron-master, who died October 25th, 1840, aged 77 years." Mr. Hazledine was the contractor for the iron work used in the construction of that surprising proof of human ingenuity, the Menai Bridge, and many other large undertakings. When our immortal sculptor, Sir Francis Chantrey, was in Shrewsbury, Jan. 7th, 1841, he visited this Church, in company with a reverend gentleman of this town, erudite in the fine arts, to whom he remarked "that in his studio the bust of Mr. Hazledine was used to be looked upon by him, with pleasure, as the very best effort of his chisel, and he felt sorry that a work he considered as one of his choice productions should be placed in such a light as to show it to the worst advantage."

On each side of the entrance leading to the chancel are tablets, highly enriched with sculpture, recording the decease of the Rev. George Scott, of Betton Strange, in this parish, and of Lucretia Ann, his wife; also of Richard Scott, of Peniarth Ucha, Merionethshire, and Underdale, in the county of Salop.

On the east wall of the chancel is a small tablet in memory of

The Rev. THOMAS STEDMAN, M.A.
"Forty-two years Vicar of this Parish, during which period
his mind, his writings, and his discourse
were with deep humility devoted
to the glory of God, the happiness of mankind,
and the temporal and spiritual interests of his flock."
He died Dec. 5th, 1825, in the 80th year of his age.

On the opposite side, a similar one records the decease of the Rev. James Edward Compson, M.A. Vicar of St. Chad's, who died at Torquay, 28th Dec. 1834, aged 40; at the base of which are the armorial bearings of the deceased.

On a large Grecian tablet is a Latin inscription to the memory of the late Rev. Francis Leighton, M.A. who died Sept. 7th, 1813, aged 66 years.*

The body of the church is 100 feet in diameter, and the total length, including the entrance and vestibule, 160 feet. It will comfortably accommodate a congregation of upwards of 2000 persons. The total cost, including site, organ, bells, &c. was £19,352, of which £15,800 was raised under act of parliament, more than one half of which still remains as a debt upon the parish.

In the vestry is a fine carved statue of St. Chad, the patron Saint, in his episcopal habit, holding a bible in his right hand and a crosier in his left. This originally stood upon the organ in the old church. A few years ago there was an order made by the trustees to place this statue over the entrance within the inner vestibule of the church, a

---

* He was a gentleman of warm piety and extensive benevolence; as a scholar and linguist he was scarcely surpassed by any of his contemporaries. He meditated a History of Shropshire, which, had it been completed, it is probable the world would have seen, from his diffusive acquirements and general antiquarian knowledge, a very superior topographical work.

position appropriate and nearly accordant to that which it occupied in the ancient fabric.

St. Chad was born in Northumberland, and exercised the greatest part of his ministry in Mercia, and, when Shrewsbury was wrested out of the hands of the Native Britons, about 775, by King Offa, the site of the Prince's Palace was soon afterwards chosen to build a Church upon, which was dedicated to this Saint, who was Bishop of Lichfield, A.D. 669. He died on the 2d of March, 672, and is said to have been canonized in the year 779. He was a Prelate of a pious and unambitious character, and held in high estimation by the people, having greatly advanced the prosperity of the Christian cause, and of this particular diocese.

The excellency of his character is pleasingly noticed in an ancient Homily, wherein it is mentioned that Theodore, having found the Bishop in the habit of undertaking pedestrian journeys far above his strength to preach the Gospel, "mounted him with his own hand on horseback, because he found him a very holy man," and insisted also on his using a *horse-man*, if the case required.—*Vide Bibl. Bodl. MSS. Junii.* 21, *Hom.* i.

The steeple is one hundred and fifty feet in height, and contains a full and melodious peal of twelve bells, the weight of the tenor being two tons one hundred weight, and measures sixteen feet six inches in circumference at the mouth: the tone is remarkably fine. The balcony beneath the dome commands a beautiful prospect of the town and distant country.

On the Bells are the following mottos, written by the late Mr. James Wilding, of College Hill:—

Treble, weight 6 cwt. 2 qrs. 25 lbs.
In sweetest sound let each its note reveal ;
Mine shall be first to lead the dulcet peal.

6 cwt. 1 qr. 14 lbs.
The public rais'd us with a liberal hand :
We come with harmony to cheer the land.

6 cwt. 3 qrs. 13 lbs.
Wide through the air extend each generous theme ;
And float melodious down Sabrina's stream.

6 cwt. 3 qrs. 0 lbs.
When female Virtue weds with manly worth,
We catch the rapture, and we spread it forth.

7 cwt. 2 qrs. 13 lbs.
Does Battle rage ? do sanguine foes contend ?
We hail the Victor, if he's—Britain's friend.

8 cwt. 0 qrs. 16 lbs.
Here let us pause, and now with one accord
Salute the Church, triumphant in the Lord.

10 cwt. 0 qrs. 10 lbs.
May George long reign, who now the sceptre sways,
And British valour ever rule the seas !

12 cwt. 1 qr. 3 lbs.
Success attend our gallant host in arms ;
And glory crown the brave whom honour warms!*

* This bell was replaced in 1836.—" W. R. Ward, J. Woodward, H. Pidgeon, R. M. Healing, Churchwardens. J. Yardley, Vicar."

13 cwt. 3 qrs. 23 lbs.
May ENGLAND'S coasts the pride of Commerce be,
And SALOP'S pride be always to be free!

16 cwt. 2 qrs. 21 lbs.
May Peace return to bless BRITANNIA'S shore,
And Faction fall to raise her head no more.

24 cwt. 1 qr. 5 lb.
May each subscriber in these numbers live,
And UNIONS ever feel those joys they give.

42 cwt. 1 qr. 0 lbs.
May all whom I shall summon to the grave
The blessings of a well-spent life receive.

Around the Tenor is the following inscription :—

"St. Chad's peal of twelve bells was cast in 1798 ;—the Rev. T. Stedman, minister ; T. Jones, A. Drinkwater, W. Harley, R. Lloyd, churchwardens. The tenor having been found ineffective, was exchanged for this bell, 1825 ;—the Rev. T. Stedman, minister ; T. Mears, of London, fecit ; S. Tudor, P. Hughes, T. Jones, C. T. Clarke, church-wardens."—As a proof of skill and perseverence, it may be mentioned that a peal of grandsire caters was rung here on April 5, 1808, in six hours and fifty minutes, containing 10,007 changes, on ten bells.

St. Chad's is considered the principal church of the town ; it is used on all public occasions, and is the place where the Archdeacon holds his visitations and probate court.

A lecture is delivered here every Thursday evening, according to a bequest of the late James Phillips, Esq. of London, who, by his will, dated 1661, devises, after the death of his wife, the rents of his property in Three Crown Court, Southwark, unto the Mayor and Aldermen of this town, for that purpose ; and also for a lecture in the parish churches of Oswestry, Ellesmere, and Whitchurch. This property now produces a good revenue, and gives to each of the lecturers a stipend of seventy pounds per annum, leaving a considerable surplus for the purchase of flannel, &c. to the poor of the above-named places. By the Municipal Act, the distribution of the proceeds of the estate rests with the Trustees of the Shrewsbury Borough Charities.

The living is a Vicarage, in the gift of the Crown, being endowed in 1674 by the benefaction of Nathaniel Tench, Esq. with the "Tythes of corn and hay of the grange of Crow Meole," which originally belonged to the church, but had become alienated. In commemoration of this gift, the testator directed that a sermon should be annually preached by the vicar on the 6th of June, which is always observed.

In conclusion, it may be mentioned that half a century having elapsed in the year 1838 since the fall of the old church of St. Chad, an event which excited great consternation, and is still had in remembrance as a remarkable interposition of Divine Providence from having happened at a time when not a single person was within reach of any injury from it, the Rev. J. Yardley, M.A. Vicar of St. Chad's, took occasion to allude to the circumstance in an appropriate discourse, which was listened to with deep attention ; and the well-timed observations will not soon be forgotten, especially when it is remembered that the original church of St. Chad, in this town, was erected at a period when the iron hand of tyranny, as practised in the late ages of the Romish church, had not blinded the eyes and exercised its arbitrary dominion over the minds of the people,—that here the dawning light of the Reformation first spread its cheering beams,—and here the exercise of the Protestant religion was first practised in Shrewsbury.

The present remains are no less instructive, and though there is scarcely a stone to remind us of the edifice raised by the Mercian King of the eighth century,—though time has not moulded into beauty the fragment that remains of a still later structure,—memory will fondly call to mind the actions of the WISE, the GOOD, and the BRAVE, who repose

in silence on the site, and excite an admonitory interest
with the " Son of the winged days," over whose fallen
habitation we tread.

JOHN EDDOWES, PRINTER.

ADDITIONS.

St. Mary's.—The patronage of this living has been vested by the Lord Chancellor in the following Trustees:—The Lord Bishop of Lichfield, the Viscount Clive, Sir A. V. Corbet, Bart. J. A. LLoyd, Esq. and R. A. Slaney, Esq. The qualification for the Minister remains as before.

Abbey Church.—The font, supported upon the upper part of an ancient cross (page 74), has been lately removed to St. Giles's Church.

St. Giles's Church.—Pews have been erected on the South side of this edifice, to correspond with those on the North.

St. George's.—A district has lately been assigned to this church, comprising the township of Frankwell.

County Hall.—Owing to a recent alteration in the arrangement of offices, it will be necessary at page 115, line 13, to *dele* to the left, and read to the right; and, at line 15, for right read left; line 17, for resting over, read towards High Street is an Entrance, &c.

ERRATA.

Page 13, for Scott read Dyer; p. 17, for Thomson read Cowper; p. 24, in note, for opposite read towards; p. 47, l. 25, for munficence read munificence; p. 58, l. 11, for surmounts read surrounds; p. 60, l. 13, for carved read coved; p. 93, l. 27, for five read four; p. 99, for Henry Edwards read Hugh Edwards; p. 127, for four read eight; p. 179, l. 15, for Sir Philip read Sir Henry.